Government: Whose Obedient Servant?

A Primer in Public Choice

Gordon Tullock
Arthur Seldon
Gordon L. Brady

D0870380

Published by The Institute of Economic Affairs,
2000

330.15
T929

First published in August 2000 by
The Institute of Economic Affairs
2 Lord North Street
Westminster
London SW1P 3LB

HB
846. B
.T85
2000

© The Institute of Economic Affairs 2000

IEA Readings 51
All rights reserved
ISBN 0-255 36482-2
ISSN 0305-814X

Many IEA publications are translated into
languages other than English or are reprinted.
Permission to translate or to reprint should
be sought from the General Director at the
address above.

Printed in Great Britain by
Hartington Fine Arts Limited, Lancing,
West Sussex
Set in Times Roman 11.5 on 12 point

Contents

University Libraries
Carnegie Mellon University
Pittsburgh PA 15213-3890

iii

EDITORIAL NOTE

In 1978 the Institute of Economic Affairs arranged a seminal event – a conference about the then relatively new subject of public choice economics, or 'the economics of politics' as it was more usually known in Britain. Papers were given by some of the key researchers in the field, including James Buchanan, and the proceedings were subsequently published in a volume[1] which became the principal reference source for economists wishing to understand the theory.

The Economics of Politics had a profound effect on IEA publications. It provided a firmer grounding for the idea, which can be found in the Institute's publications from the beginning, that it is inconsistent, in a subject which claims to follow scientific method, to seek out and emphasise market 'imperfections' and 'failures' whilst disregarding government failure. The ideas of the public choice school have so permeated the Institute's publications that virtually every monograph has for many years had those ideas at its heart. Whether it is a study of a general issue, such as government regulation, or of a particular market, Institute authors have, when making policy recommendations, kept firmly in mind the imperfections of political and bureaucratic action. They have thus distanced themselves from the idea, still implicit in much economic policy analysis, that government action will invariably improve on the market outcome.

For some years *The Economics of Politics* has been out of print and, of course, the subject has moved on considerably in the last twenty years. Other general monographs on public choice analysis have been published by the IEA[2]. But the time is clearly right for a new reference book on public choice which presents its main ideas without excessive technical jargon. The Institute has been fortunate to persuade three leading exponents to write it. Professor Gordon Tullock is one of the founding fathers of public choice theory and has been responsible for many of the

---

[1]   James M. Buchanan et al., *The Economics of Politics*, Readings 18, Institute of Economic Affairs, 1978.

[2]   For example, *Government As It Is*, William C. Mitchell, Hobart Paper 109, Institute of Economic Affairs, 1988

most imaginative ideas and the most significant advances in the subject; Dr. Arthur Seldon, for many years the IEA's Editorial Director, was one of the first to recognise the importance of public choice and has been one of the principal contributors to the development of the subject in Britain since it was first opened up to study; and Dr. Gordon Brady has written extensively about the way in which the theory can be applied in different markets. As a bonus for readers, there is a Foreword to the book by Sir Antony Jay, joint author of the *Yes, Minister* and *Yes, Prime Minister* series which opened many peoples' eyes to the ways of politicians and civil servants and offered most perceptive guidance to the incentives which govern their behaviour.

All IEA publications contain the views of their authors, not those of the Institute (which has no corporate view), its Trustees, Advisers or Directors. *Government: Whose Obedient Servant?* is published as a major contribution to public understanding of how economic analysis can illuminate the workings of governments.

July 2000

Colin Robinson
Editorial Director, Institute of Economic Affairs
Professor of Economics, University of Surrey

FOREWORD

In 1977, when I first had the idea for a television comedy series based on the tension and conflicts between a cabinet minister and his Permanent Secretary – we later called it *Yes, Minister* – I had never heard of Public Choice Economics. I had, however, as a writer and producer (and sometime member of a government committee) spent twenty years in the world of television current affairs and seen the system in action. The more I studied it, the wider I realised the gap was between the projected image of government and the reality; in particular, the image of all-powerful ministers telling their civil servants what to do and the reality of civil servants more or less controlling all but the most powerful, energetic and intelligent ministers. The most telling example was an incident in the early 1960s. It had become clear that the hanging of Timothy Evans had been a grave miscarriage of justice, and a petition for his posthumous free pardon received a huge number of signatures. The appeal was led by Labour's Shadow Home Secretary, Sir Frank Soskice. It was presented to the Home Secretary and rejected. Nothing unusual about that – except that there had just been a general election, and the Home Secretary who rejected the petition was the same Sir Frank Soskice who had organised it. It was a delicious insight into the true balance of power between ministers and civil servants, and indeed between individuals and institutions.

This gap between the image and the reality created a wonderful space for comedy, and it had the vital ingredient of conflict – conflict between the minister who was desperate for favourable publicity, promotion (or avoidance of sacking) and re-election for himself and his party, and the Permanent Secretary who was obsessed with status, security, risk avoidance, freedom from objective measurement of his performance, increasing his department's budget and authority, comfort, leisure, perks, a good income and a KCB. The comedy derived not only from the conflict but also from the cloak of public interest and service with which they were obliged to cover the nakedness of their ambitions. Their protestations of exclusive concern for the good of the country and its citizens were reminiscent of Emerson's line. 'The louder he talked of his honour, the faster we counted the spoons'.

Jonathan Lynn, my co-author, and I spent the best part of ten years on the two series, *Yes Minister* and *Yes, Prime Minister*. Each of the 38 episodes was based on research lunches with people who had worked in the top levels of government. Civil servants tended to be distressingly discreet, but ministers, ex-ministers and political advisers were wonderfully forthcoming. The more we learnt, the more we realised that had we been in the same position as our fictional minister and Permanent Secretary, Jim Hacker and Sir Humphrey Appleby, we would probably have behaved exactly as they did. The problem was not the quality or morality of the individuals, it was the system of rewards and penalties within which they had to work. Our evidence was personal and anecdotal and it has been fascinating to see in *Government: Whose Obedient Servant?* how a scholarly discipline has given academic corroboration to our personal insights. It explodes the myth that people in public service are secular saints, sacrificing self interest on the altar of public service, by contrast with the rest of us who are squalid money-grubbers and profit-chasers. They are no better and no worse than the rest of us, but the organisational system and moral climate they work in makes it impossible for them to admit it.

If anything was quite irrefutably clear from our ten years' research, it was that the public good is not the objective of government: it is a constraint. Unless their activities are perceived or believed to be in the public interest, there will be retribution, so some of their time (and all their rhetoric) has to be devoted to furthering it, or claiming to have furthered it. But as this book shows, the theory that things are better done by government officials than private citizens or companies is simply not sustainable. I see no way of reforming the system, so the only sensible course is to leave to government only those tasks which it is impossible to have done in any other way – a view which any reader of this admirable book will find it hard to disagree with.

July 2000

Sir Antony Jay
Langport, Somerset

THE AUTHORS

Gordon Tullock received his J.D. (University of Chicago, 1947) and an honorary Ph.D. (University of Chicago, 1994). He is a Distinguished Fellow of the American Economic Association (1998). He has been a major contributor to the development of the theoretical underpinnings of public choice. Tullock's hypotheses, Tullock's laws, and Tullock's paradoxes have shaped the development of public choice, as well as charting new areas in law and economics and sociobiology. Beginning with his initial publications in the *Journal of Political Economy* and the *American Economic Review,* Tullock has published over 160 articles (not counting reprints and translations), 130 communications, and 20 books. For the IEA he contributed papers to *The Economics of Charity* (IEA Readings No. 12, 1974), *The Taming of Government* (IEA Readings No. 21, 1979), and *The Emerging Consensus* (Hobart Paperback No. 14, 1981), as well as his essay on public choice/the economics of politics entitled *The Vote Motive* (Hobart Paperback No. 9, 1976). Tullock is currently Professor of Law and Economics at George Mason University School of Law, Arlington, Virginia.

Arthur Seldon was educated at Raine's Foundation School and the London School of Economics, where he graduated with a first class honours degree in economics. He has been a university tutor and examiner in economics, an economist in industry, special adviser to a Cabinet Committee on Welfare of the Commonwealth of Australia, and a member of a British Medical Association advisory panel on health service financing. He was Editorial Director of the Institute of Economic Affairs, 1957–88. His scholarly writings include some 230 essays in 74 newspapers and periodicals. His longer works, apart from writing 28 papers and books, and editing 350 papers at the IEA, include: *Everyman's Dictionary of Economics* with F. G. Pennance (J. M. Dent), *The Great Pensions Swindle* (Stacey), *Charge* (Temple Smith), *Capitalism* (Blackwell), *The State is Rolling Back* (Economic and Literary Books), and *The Dilemma of Democracy* (IEA).

Gordon L. Brady received his Ph.D. from Virginia Polytechnic Institute and State University (1976) and a Masters in the Study of Law from Yale Law School (1981). Author of over 70 publications, he is currently writing an intellectual biography of Duncan Black and a history of the Thomas Jefferson Center for Studies in Political Economy. He was an Associate Fellow at The Royal Institute of International Affairs in London and is now a Senior Research Associate at the Center for Study of Public Choice, George Mason University, Fairfax, Va. Previous posts include Senior Advisor for Environmental Economics, Bureau of International Organization Affairs, US Department of State, Washington, D.C.; Senior Economic Policy Advisor, President's Council on Environmental Quality, Washington, D.C. Trent Fellow in the Department of Economics and Social Science at Nottingham Trent University; Graduate Fellow at Yale Law School and Lecturer in Economics, Yale University; Economic Policy Fellow, The Brookings Institution, Washington, D.C.; and Rockefeller Post-Doctoral Fellow in Environmental Affairs, Law & Economics Center, University of Miami. From 1998–99, he was Director of the Law & Economics Center, George Mason University School of Law, Arlington, Virginia.

ACKNOWLEDGEMENTS
The authors wish to acknowledge helpful comments from Alden F. Abbott, US Department of Commerce; Mark Brady, George Mason University, Fairfax, Va.; Charles K. Rowley, Locke Institute, Fairfax, Va.; and Richard E. Wagner, Department of Economics, George Mason University, Fairfax, Va.

INTRODUCTION

Arthur Seldon

MANY ECONOMIC WRITERS AND TEACHERS still present economic systems of exchange between private individuals or firms as 'imperfect' and requiring 'correction' by government. Most teachers of politics, politicians and political journalists still present government as well-meaning and able to remove the 'imperfections'. The common refrain in everyday conversation and in 'Letters to the Editor' that some goods and services are faulty is followed by the conclusion that 'the government ought to put a stop to it'.

The economists and the political commentators, with rare exceptions, have been mistaken and misleading. Economic systems based on exchange between individuals and selling and buying between firms usually correct themselves in time if they are free to adapt themselves to changing conditions of supply and demand. Government 'cures' usually do more harm than good in the long run because of three stubborn and too long neglected excesses of government: their 'cures' are begun too soon, they do too much, and they are continued too long. Once a government cure is introduced it stays for years or decades. Anti-trust law to prevent or end monopoly is continued long after the monopoly has been ended by technical invention or other cures.

This is the lesson of this book on the connections between economics and politics.

Political scientists and practitioners have been wrong long enough. And economists have been too slow in applying economics to the politics of government.

Abraham Lincoln's encouraging vision of 'government of the people, by the people, for the people' raised hopes that have never been realised. But his name can no longer be used to justify the error that he could not have foreseen in 1863. He could not have envisaged that, a century after he was assassinated, government in the United

States of America, and even more in Great Britain and Europe, would dominate economic life. If he had survived he would not now have approved of the dominant government that democracy has produced. For it is no longer 'of' the people, 'by' the people, 'for' the people.

The application of economics to politics reveals a form of government that Lincoln would not have commended in 1900, 1945, or in 2000. Government is now very different from that based on the common people which Lincoln thought it would become. Although his vision is still the most common encyclopaedia definition of 'democracy' he cannot now be claimed as the father of our 20th–21st century form of democracy.

Lincoln would now see government not 'of', 'by' and 'for' all the people but 'of', 'by' and 'for' some kinds of people. He would see it not as 'of' all the people but of the political activists. He would see government not as 'by' the people but as managed by the politicians and their officials. And he would see government not as 'for' the ordinary people but as 'for' the organised in well-run, well-financed, and influential business organisations, professional associations and trade unions. It is government 'of the Busy (political activists), by the Bossy (government managers), for the Bully (lobbying activists)'.

This Readings is intended as an introduction (or 'Primer') for newcomers – students and the general public – to the latest developments in the study of government that rules much of their lives. It uses the tools of economics to judge 'politics' – the ability or failure of collective action by 'representatives' elected by people as voters to serve them as users or consumers of the goods and services they may least prefer. It thus examines how, or how well, or how poorly, government of perhaps 100 or 500 'representatives' that appears to be chosen by the collective public to provide 'public choice' can satisfy the widely differing choices of the people as millions of individuals.

Is the election of even 500 people in a political assembly by the 'public choice' of the people as voters capable of satisfying the individual choices of the millions?

This subject is also taught to students by abstract reasoning and advanced mathematics. Here the authors use everyday language and a little simple arithmetic. This simple introduction can later be supplemented by more advanced texts indicated in the references.

This new approach was developed by two American economists some 40 years ago and is widely taught in American universities. But it is still comparatively rarely known in Britain by the teachers or students of other social sciences or by commentators on political events.

The Institute saw the importance of public choice in its early years. There had always been acute discussion and criticism – and condemnation – of 'private' choice by people as individuals or in families and various voluntary groupings. But the discussion of 'public' choice – choices by political people with power over the lives of other people – was uncommon.

From the early 1960s onwards, the IEA published writings by the two founders of 'public' choice, Professors James Buchanan and Gordon Tullock, both with significantly Scottish names as though to acknowledge affinity with the 18th-century Scottish giants of philosophy and economics, David Hume and Adam Smith. And both 20th-century Scottish Americans developed their revolutionary thinking on public choice most recently at George Mason University in the Commonwealth of Virginia that derived its name from the English Queen Elizabeth I (the 'virgin queen').

Four IEA papers typified their contribution to original economic thinking throughout the life of the IEA. The first publication, in 1965, emerged from Professor Buchanan's observation at a discussion of the National Health Service that its incurable underlying dilemma was that the people would not pay in taxes for as much (or as good) medical care as they desired or expected 'free' from government. Then, as still in our day, the explanation by sociologists and political scientists, that the cause was 'under-funding', was based on the continuing preoccupation with macro-economic rather than micro-economic thinking.[1]

---

[1] J. M. Buchanan, *The Inconsistencies of the National Health Service*, IEA Occasional Paper No. 7, London: Institute of Economic Affairs, 1965.

The second of the four characteristic public choice publications came from Professor Tullock with a Hobart Paperback in 1976, entitled *The Vote Motive* in contrast to the pre-occupation with 'the profit motive' by the critics of 'commercial' buying and selling between individual people or private groups.[2] The Commentary by Morris Perlman of the London School of Economics, the home of post-war sociological confusion, emphasised the fundamental importance of the argument that the vote motive in government often produced the wrong results, and it drew the admission from a journal of the producers of 'public choice', the *Municipal Journal*, that 'Professor Tullock's disturbing tract deserves our attention'.

The third public choice event, described by the title preferred by the IEA as 'The Economics of Politics', was a two-day conference in 1978 opened by Professor Buchanan with contributions by economists from Canada, America and Switzerland. Among the many challenging issues raised were 'Can Majority Voting Express the Public Interest?', 'Are Civil Servants Economic Eunuchs?', and 'Can Constitutions Control Governments?'.[3]

And the fourth publication that now raises these and other major issues in the politics of democracy is this 'Primer in Public Choice' – a restatement of central principles, with illustrations of how 'public choice' in practice, in everyday government, in Britain and America (and every other country and continent) can operate *against* the public choices of the people.

Both Professors Buchanan and Tullock have contributed to further IEA discussions. Professor Buchanan, with the American Professor R.E. Wagner and the British Professor John Burton, wrote in 1978 a decisive rejection of Keynesian thinking on government budgetary policies[4] and a further *Hobart Paper* (No. 88) in 1981 with the Australian Professor Geoffrey Brennan on the fatal tendency of

---

[2] Gordon Tullock, *The Vote Motive*, Hobart Paperback No. 9, 1976.

[3] J. M. Buchanan *et al.*, *The Economics of Politics*, IEA Readings No. 18, 1978.

[4] J. M. Buchanan, R. E. Wagner and John Burton, *The Consequences of Mr Keynes*, Hobart Paper No. 78, 1978.

governments to debase the coinage and engineer inflation to maintain their revenues.[5]

And Professor Tullock's further contributions were a paper at an IEA conference on 'The Taming of Government' chaired by Professor Lord Robbins in 1979,[6] a contribution to a symposium of papers on 'The Economics of Charity' in 1974,[7] and a collection of long-term essays on 'The Emerging Consensus' in 1981.[8]

Primer in Public Choice – Main Propositions

This Primer in Public Choice is now intended as a concise collection in three parts by three authors to re-assert and illustrate some of the main propositions of public choice. The principles are outlined by Professor Tullock, the illustrations from North America are written by Dr Gordon Brady, and the demonstrations in Britain by the writer of this Introduction. The Notes on Authors indicates their varying background and activities.

The Primer is a compact assembly of the material envisaged in a longer work begun by Professor Tullock, Professor Charles Rowley, newly arrived at George Mason University from the University of Newcastle-upon-Tyne but a previous contributor to IEA Papers, and the under-signed. We met in 1986 for a month at GMU to prepare the longer study and began to discuss and judge early drafts as the preparation for further work, beginning with the early English and French mathematicians who had explored the faults of voting systems and much else. Increasing commitments required by GMU, editorship of the journal *Public Choice* and other activities obliged Professor Rowley, with our regret, to withdraw from the Primer, which had then to be deferred until a replacement could be found. Dr Brady finally emerged as an economist who had worked on aspects of public choice, including

---

[5] H. Geoffrey Brennan and James M. Buchanan, *Monopoly in Money and Inflation*, Hobart Paper No. 88, 1981.

[6] *The Taming of Government*, IEA Readings No. 21, 1979.

[7] *The Economics of Charity*, IEA Readings No. 12, 1974.

[8] *The Emerging Consensus...?*, Hobart Paperback No. 14, 1981.

the editing of a volume of Professor Tullock's unpublished writings. We are grateful to Professor Rowley for sharing our early discussions and inspiring much that appears in the present book.

Professor Tullock now presents some main principles of public choice in simple language and elementary arithmetic. Dr Brady's Part II clarifies the technical language used in the American science-based industries to show the likely results of closer government controls over the Internet and other enterprising new industries.

Part III assesses the arguments and doubts in the continued British government control or regulation of industries and of services in the welfare state that have become outdated by general economic advance and accelerated invention: the new aspirations for higher standards by parents in education, by patients in medical care, by families in housing and by retired employees in pensions.

Since the original authors would be discussing, and in parts questioning, long-accepted notions of the benevolence of 'democracy' and other unquestioned aspects of Western government, they visited the site of the July 1863 Battle of Gettysburg where Abraham Lincoln had voiced the sentiments that have long sustained the hopes of mankind, but dimmed the judgement, of the historic promise: 'government of the people, by the people, for the people.'

On the site of the military action that may have decided the outcome of the battle, and therefore perhaps the future of American democracy, Professor Tullock's prodigious memory pointed to the slight gradient in the field across which the soldiers of the Confederacy had charged to meet the over-powering fire of the guns of the Union.

The coming years will show whether the power of government to enforce its political laws, rules, regulations, and other devices will prevail over the increasing power of the people to abolish remaining scarcities and prefer to enrich one another by the economic 'laws' of exchange decided by themselves in the light of new freedoms that enable them to escape from outdated government.

PART I

THE THEORY OF
PUBLIC CHOICE

Gordon Tullock

PEOPLE ARE PEOPLE:

THE ELEMENTS OF PUBLIC CHOICE

'Homo politicus and *homo economicus* are the same. The critical implication of this assumption of universal self-interest is that the observed differences between public choices and private choices emerge not because individuals adopt different behavioral objectives in the two settings, but rather because the constraints on behavior are different. Different outcomes emerge not because public choices are guided by motives different from those guiding private choices, but rather because in private markets self-interested voters and politicians make choices that mainly affect themselves, while in political markets self-interested voters and politicians make choices that mainly affect others.'[1]

Political Actors and the 'Public Interest'

PUBLIC CHOICE IS A SCIENTIFIC ANALYSIS OF GOVERNMENT BEHAVIOUR and, in particular, the behaviour of individuals with respect to government. Strictly speaking, it has no policy implications except that in some cases it might be demonstrated that a particular policy is impossible or extremely unlikely to achieve its stated policy goals. For example, students of public choice would not be particularly impressed with a policy of 'maximising the public interest' and would recognise the inherent difficulties of obtaining free trade or achieving a balanced budget in seven years. They would regard these policy objectives as rather like telling the pilot of a Boeing 747 to get to London faster than the Concorde.

---

[1] F. S. McChesney and W. F. Shughart II, *The Causes and Consequences of Antitrust: The Public Choice Perspective*, Chicago: The University of Chicago Press, 1995, pp. 9–10.

Until the days of Adam Smith (1723–1790),[2] most social discussion was essentially moral. Individuals – whether they were businessmen, civil servants, politicians, or hereditary monarchs – were told what was the morally correct thing to do and urged to do it. It was implicitly assumed that all these people should be, and perhaps were, engaged in maximising the public interest. Machiavelli (1469–1527)[3] and Hobbes (1588–1679)[4] were major exceptions to this rule; nevertheless, in both cases their influence was much less than their readership might suggest. They were taken by most of their readers as wickedly arguing against morality, rather than producing a scientific system which was essentially amoral.

David Hume (1711–1776)[5] was the first to make significant cracks in this monolithic approach. He took the rather obvious view that most people pursued their own interest in their behaviour rather than a broadly based public interest, and in several essays applied this line of reasoning to economics. Forerunners to his work can be found in European and, indeed, non-European thought. But, until the time of Hume and his friend, Adam Smith, the prevailing view of human nature and government was that the moral or public interest approach was dominant. Adam Smith developed modern economics by assuming that individuals were very largely self-interested and working out the consequences of that assumption in the realm of economics. In *The Nature and Causes of the Wealth of Nations*, Smith devoted three chapters to government, while retaining the moralistic or public-interest model.

From the time of Plato (428–347BC)[6] and Aristotle (384–322)[7] political science was viewed simply as a matter of producing morally

---

[2] See Adam Smith's *The Nature and Causes of the Wealth of Nations* (1776). There are many editions.

[3] Nicolo Machiavelli, *The Prince* (1532) (many editions).

[4] Thomas Hobbes, *Leviathan* (1650) (many editions).

[5] David Hume, *Esssays Moral and Political* (1741–42) (many editions).

[6] Plato, *The Republic* (many editions).

[7] Aristotle, *Politics* (many editions).

correct policies. The claim by Leo Strauss (1899–1973)[8] that political science was 'the science of right action' was extreme, but not untypical. There was no formal theory of how government works outside such moral and ethical foundations.

Throughout the 19th and well into the 20th century, economists assumed that individuals are primarily concerned with their own interest and worked out the consequences of that assumption. On the other hand, during this same period political science largely assumed that political actors are mainly concerned with the public interest. Thus, an individual who enters a supermarket and purchases items of his choice is assumed, when he enters the voting booth, to vote *not* for the politicians and laws which will benefit him, but for politicians and laws which will benefit the nation as a whole. The person in the supermarket mainly buys the food and other goods that are, granted their price, found to benefit him and his family.[9] However, once he becomes a politician, a transformation is assumed to occur so that a broader perspective guides him to make morally correct decisions rather than follow the course of behaviour which pleases the interest groups which supported him or the policies which may lead to re-election.

The Bifurcated View of Human Behaviour

Economists changed this bifurcated view of human behaviour by developing the theory of public choice which amounts, in essence, to transplanting the general analytical framework of economics into political science. The statement that the voter in the voting booth is the same person as the customer in the supermarket does not seem radical, but is nevertheless a very dramatic change from the political science literature. Indeed, the author of this Part I has often been denounced with great vigour at professional meetings by conventional political scientists for expounding this view.

---

[8] Leo Strauss; almost any one of his books.

[9] He may, and most people do, make charitable contributions from time to time. These are usually a fairly small part (5 per cent or so) of his total income.

This bifurcation of the individual psyche is particularly impressive when it is remembered that the economic system based upon self-interest assumptions can be demonstrated to produce a result not totally out of accord with the classical ideas of the public interest. On the other hand, until very recently, there was no proof that the government would generate an output in accord with the classical ideas of public interest. Indeed, the first demonstration that the government might tend to produce an outcome which, in any sense, was optimal came from people who adopted economic assumptions about political behaviour.

Since the *same* people engage in market activities and in politics, it seems simpler to assume that their behaviour has the same motivation in both of these areas. Indeed, it is rather difficult to understand how the bifurcated view of individual behaviour has been maintained. Nevertheless, it has been and remains the dominant view. Of course, empirical confirmation of any theoretical proposition is more important than analytical elegance. Most people realise that when considering the behaviour of any individual politician, he behaves in a self-interested way, and similarly, when considering the factors that affect votes, most people assume that personal gain is certainly an aspect.

The politician in a democratic society is a man who makes a living by winning elections. This rather simple and obvious observation seems to have escaped the early students of government. To quote an American aphorism: 'In order to be a great Senator, one must, first of all, be a Senator.' In other words, those people whom we elect to office are there because they are good at being elected. This characteristic of periodic re-assessment makes them similar in many ways to the business man. Just as a business man designs, let us say, the latest automobile so as to attract customers, the politician selects policies with the idea that his customer, the voter, will reward him in the next election. No one considers this activity as absolutely wicked, but it is, in general, not an exercise in the application of some high-level moral principle. Politicians and businessmen will sometimes pay a price (lost constituent support) in order to do what they think is good, but on the whole they can be expected to act in such a way as to maximise their own well-being in terms of re-election prospects.

Stated in different language, the politician as business man pursues policies which he thinks the people want because he hopes they will reward him with their votes. To say that the voters actually rule under this scheme is not a bad approximation. Nor is this from the standpoint of democracy particularly undesirable.

Politics and the Information Problem

In considering the consequences of this simple view of government, there is one special problem: economists have based their predictions on the notion that purchasers in the market are perfectly informed.[10] Unfortunately, in the case of politics the information problem is much worse than it is in the market. Consider the following example of individual behavioural incentives in a private market choice. In purchasing an automobile I invest a certain amount of time and resources in learning about new cars, for the simple reason that I know a mistake will directly affect me, my wallet, convenience, and comfort.

But, when voting for the president of the United States, my vote will be one of 70 million cast and is highly unlikely to affect the final outcome of the election. This realisation can be expected to affect the valuation which I place on my vote and the resources that I will invest to collect information to make a 'correct' choice. This means that politicians trying to select policies that will attract voters know that the voters will put much less energy into trying to make a correct choice than they would when purchasing an automobile or some other item whose shortcomings and advantages will accrue to them alone. The voters are, therefore, likely to be badly informed and may favour a politician or policies that are directly contrary to their interest. From the standpoint of the individual candidate, what is

---

[10] The reason may be the development of the mathematical theory of perfect competition in which if you assume that people are perfectly informed, the mathematics is easier than if you assume they have the kind of information they really do have. The more modern theory of economics argues that people accumulate information as long as the value of more information will exceed its cost. However, the decision about collecting information is made at a time when they do not know the value of additional information in terms of what advantages it would provide.

important is what the people want given their perception of the value of their vote on the outcome and the cost of becoming informed, *not* what they would want if they were better informed.

The same is true for designers of automobiles, but they know that their customers will be, if not perfectly informed, at least better informed than the voter. Putting it briefly, I get a positive return on additional information when I am buying a car because it will improve my choice. Frequent and costly repairs and the inconvenience of being stranded on a cold and lonely highway waiting for a tow truck are in my self-interest to avoid. Automobile designers know this, and hence design cars with the intention of attracting reasonably informed customers. But when I vote I am aware that my vote will have almost no effect on the kind of policies I shall get. This result occurs because the policies and politicians chosen will be determined to a much greater extent by the votes of other people. Politicians once again know this, and hence attempt to design policies which will attract ill-informed voters.

This limited information on general topics contrasts with the much greater knowledge most people have about specific policies. Consider the following examples: farmers know a great deal about farm subsidies and acreage limitations (in the United States and in Europe); workers and management are well-informed about import restrictions on goods which directly compete with those they manufacture. This asymmetrical information bias leads to the emergence of special-interest groups and encourages politicians to pay attention to them.

Democratic Versus Non-Democratic Government

It is important to issue a special note of warning. In this *Primer* we will discuss at length the defects of the government in a democratic process; however, it does not mean that we know a better way to deal with these problems. Air pollution is normally handled ineffectively by the government, but whatever one can say about the defects of the air quality management controls that now exist, they *may* be better than leaving it to the market. Further experimentation with non-democratic forms of government indicates that they produce outcomes which are less desirable than democracy. As a consequence, we have a form of government which is far from what we would really like, but until a new and better one is invented, we had better keep the one we have despite its shortcomings. Nevertheless, it is true that we should be fully aware of the difficulties and inefficiencies that are to be expected from the government. The objective of this *Primer* is more limited: We ask, what is public choice and what difference does public choice make in understanding democratic processes?

Leaving Everything to the Market?

Are students of public choice different and, if so, why? To begin, we might ask why we have government at all. The market produces many things with remarkable efficiency, but why not have the market take over everything, as recommended by economists such as Murray Rothbard (1926–1995)? The *standard* answer to this argument goes back to Hume, but in modern times it is associated with the names of economists such as A. C. Pigou (1877–1959) and Paul A. Samuelson (Nobel Laureate in Economics 1970). The problem is essentially technological. The market requires some system of property rights under which individuals are allocated power over various aspects of the real world. Individuals holding 'property' see opportunities for improving their well-being by various types of agreements with each other (as well as, of course, their individual labour), and enter into agreements, thus achieving improvements in their well-being. Unfortunately, under any known allocation of property rights, it will occasionally occur that the number of people who must agree is very large and, further (and this is a very important qualification), that the particular group which must agree is not given at the outset of the analysis.

The importance of the last criterion is fundamental. If we propose to establish a new corporation and sell stock on the stock market, we may require the concurrence of a very large number of people (buyers, sellers of other stock, regulators). But the number of people we require is a small part of all potential investors, and hence the people who will become stockholders is not prespecified. If, on the other hand, we are proposing to improve police protection in Tucson or London, the number of people who are directly concerned is determined at the outset. If we permit individuals to decide whether

9

they will pay for the police department, and given the technological conditions under which additional police protection is delivered, we would anticipate that very little police protection would be purchased. The only way out of this dilemma, assuming we have complete private property, would be to arrange a unanimous agreement under which each of us put a certain amount of money up in return for the agreement of all the others. Clearly the bargaining costs would be immense. The role of government, under the modern view, is to permit us to gain this type of an advantage, to enter into this kind of an agreement – *without* requiring unanimity, and hence obtain much lower bargaining costs.

The Costs and Benefits of Government

It will immediately be obvious that, without unanimous agreement, we must have some other method of making decisions, and it may clearly impose costs upon at least some members of the community. Thus, we would adopt government decision-making only if we anticipated that the costs to us of the bargaining eliminated are higher than the potential of being victimised by whatever decision process we choose. In this sense, government becomes a market surrogate for obtaining economic profit in areas where bargaining is costly. Looked at in this way, there is no obvious reason why the 'public interest' must be served by the government, but one can at least imagine that decision-making processes could be designed such that an outcome in a sense equivalent to the classical public interest might be achieved. It would, in other words, be somewhat like market provision. In both cases, it could be argued that the system provided something which most people would want, simply because the motivating force of the organisation is individual desires.

The student of public choice, in dealing with the government, does not expect that it will efficiently achieve the 'classical goals' of government. It does not follow that it cannot efficiently achieve *other* goals or, indeed, that with appropriate redesign, it might not achieve *some* of the classical goals, such as efficient enforcement of the law against assault and battery. Indeed, we can find many cases in which that goal of government has been carried out quite efficiently in the past or in the present. Washington, DC, in 1911, had safe streets, as does Zurich today.[11]

Government and the Pursuit of Private Interests

We must accept that in government, as in any form of commerce, people will pursue their private interests, and they will achieve goals which are reasonably closely related to those of company stockholders or of citizens only if it is in their private interest to do so. The primacy of private interest is not inconsistent with the observation that most people, in addition to pursuing their private interests, have some charitable instincts, some tendency to help others, and to engage in various morally correct activities.

However, the evidence seems fairly strong that these motives other than the pursuit of private interests are not ones on which we can depend for the achievement of long-continued efficient performance. Consider two groups, federal judges and college professors. Both groups have been granted substantially guaranteed employment with no risk of being fired. In both cases, there are a great many who take advantage of this, not to maximise the production of truth, truthful research, or correct decisions, but to maximise their enjoyment of leisure. There are tenured professors and judges who work hard; but, in both cases, the average is fairly low.[12]

Most traditional students of political science would regard such remarks as not only wrong but wicked. Indeed, it is possible that such statements about federal judges are illegal in the sense that, in theory,

---

[11] The 1911 date comes from the fact that the morning paper reported the death, as the result of a daylight mugging incident directly in front of her home, of a very elderly socialite, Gladys H. Werlich, who first moved to that address in 1911. (*Washington Post*, 21 January 1976, p. A1.)

[12] No authority is needed with respect to college professors, but for a discussion of federal judges' work habits, see G. Tullock, 'On the Efficient Organization of Trials', *Kyklos* 28, Fasc. 4, 1975, pp. 745–62; see also comment by McChesney, Ordover and Weitzman and my reply in *Kyklos*, Fasc. 30, 1977, pp. 517–19. Also 'Public Decisions as Public Goods', *Journal of Political Economy*, July/August 1971, pp. 913–18.

one could be held in contempt of court for having made them, regardless of the ability to prove their truth. But the different attitude towards government which arises from public choice does have major effects on our views on what policies government should undertake or can carry out. In particular, it makes us much less ambitious about relying on government to provide certain services. No student of public choice would feel that the establishment of a national health service in the United States would mean that the doctors would work devotedly to improve the health of the citizens. We should anticipate that, unless a very carefully designed incentive system is set up, many doctors will tend to behave rather as the British doctors have.

Public Choice and Policy Choices

Unfortunately, few students of public choice have integrated their studies of public choice into their choice of policy. Public choice is a relatively recent intellectual endeavour and most of us are subject to a great deal of advice and information about policy which comes from non-public choice sources. Further, most of us are (at least to some extent) allied with political forces, the main strength of which comes from influences aside from public choice economists.

Of course, we are far from unanimous agreement about every policy, even in those activities where public choice would be relevant. Some students of public choice try to change public choice to fit their prior conceptions, rather than *vice versa*. An example which impresses me is the continued defence of simple majority voting as a standard method of making decisions.

But so much for cases where public choice has not been integrated into the policy views of its students. Where are the areas where it has been integrated? One is simply a lack of enthusiasm for government as a solution to problems. The view that government is the automatic perfect solution to innumerable problems no longer exists. Not very long ago, the simple proof that the economy did not function perfectly was regarded as an adequate reason for governmental action. Today, we start from the knowledge that the government also does not function perfectly and make a selection between two imperfect operational devices in terms of their relative perfection and certain other characteristics, such as the distributional effect of government programmes.

Market Imperfection and Government Imperfections

This change, although it originated in the public choice field, has now spread through economics as a whole. A deep-seated feeling that government is imperfect carries with it two consequences. The *first* is that imperfections in the market process do not necessarily call for government intervention; the *second* is a desire to see if we cannot do something about government processes which might conceivably improve their efficiency (discussed in Chapter 7).

Public choice students are more likely than students of the older approaches to political matters to be in favour of shifting reliance from the government sector to the market sector. However, we must not make a mistake which is the converse of the one criticised above: that the government performs certain functions poorly does not, in and of itself, prove that the market would do better. That government and market alternatives should be compared on the same basis is a strength of public choice. As it happens, I believe there are clear cases for privatisation; but my arguments for it would have to involve a comparison of the likely inefficiency of private services with the existing inefficiency of the public services. Arguments of this sort, in which a theory is compared with a functioning entity, are always difficult.

There are many areas where the government has been called in to supplement the activity of the private market by regulation – for example, the Interstate Commerce Commission and the Federal Trade Commission in the United States. However, it has only quite recently been appreciated that such regulatory agencies might make the market work less well. It is certainly true that the market for transportation in the days when the railroad was the basic method of surface transportation worked badly in many respects. If public choice had been in existence in those days, however, I imagine that there would have been at least a few academics testifying before Congress that government cartelisation of the industry was likely to be even more imperfect.

The principal proponents of deregulation in recent years have not in general been public choice economists, but a number of them have been subject to a strong public choice influence. It is certainly true that students of public choice are apt to be in the forefront of those who want to examine critically existing regulatory agencies or proposals for further regulation.

The Design of Government

Enough has been said about the areas where public choice leads to what might be called 'a lack of enthusiasm' for the governmental solution. Let us now turn to the design of government itself and how the student of public choice might view it. Traditional political science was to a very large extent devoted to the study of democracy and discussed various forms of government, to a large extent in terms of how 'democratic' they were. Since there was no clear agreement on what 'democratic' meant, these discussions tended not to get very far. In any event, it is interesting that the idea that whatever democracy was, it was the be-all and end-all of government seems not to have been questioned until very recently. Now, partly because of the existence of the public choice paradigm, it is possible to discuss market alternatives to government in a serious and scientific way.

Another area where public choice has been important is in decisions on the location and optimal size of government units. By location, in this case, I am thinking not of geographic location but location on the hierarchy of scale. Most public choice students are in favour of much more decentralisation of government than was characteristic of the intellectuals interested in politics even 20 years ago. The development of techniques which make it possible, at least in theory, to determine what is an optimal government unit has been an important reason for this development.

The realisation that we can adjust sizes of government to fit our needs has led to another development, the very local government. I live in a collective called the Sunshine Mountain Ridge Association in the State of Arizona, where the 400 other householders (voters in this area) engage in all sorts of collective activity which traditionally would have been left to private citizens. We jointly plant trees and shrubs, regulate other gardening efforts, and the paint of the exterior of our houses. This, as readers will realise, is an illustration of a type of intervention in private life which must be expected when activities are collectivised and planned. Nevertheless, although there is clearly a cost here, there is an advantage, too. I have some control over the physical appearance of my neighbours' houses as they have over mine, and we are able to produce a better general effect than if we had not collectivised these activities in order to internalise externalities.

The Behaviour of Government Officials

A final area where knowledge of public choice has an effect on people's views about policy concerns the behaviour of government officials. The student of public choice is unlikely to believe that government officials are overly concerned with the public interest. Since they operate in an area where information is very poor (and the proof that the voters' information on political issues would be poor was one of the first achievements of the public choice theory), deception is much more likely to be a paying tactic than it is in the market-place. Therefore, one would anticipate more dishonesty in government. Indeed, granted that government officials are the only people who can check on the dishonesty of government officials, the problem of curing dishonesty in government involves an infinite regress. Private businessmen, who deal with better informed consumers than do politicians, are also subject to surveillance by public officials who, dishonest though some may be, very commonly have no personal motive to protect a particular private businessman. The amount of dishonesty which has turned up in private business in spite of these inspections gives a rough idea of the almost complete uniformity of dishonesty in politics.

Having little confidence in politicians and depending upon the electoral process to discipline them, insofar as they are disciplined, is the appropriate attitude and it leads to some feelings of cynicism about election campaigns. Moreover, there are problems of defining honesty or dishonesty. The politician who sells his decision in Congress for votes is not obviously in better moral shape than the politician who sells it for cash. Nevertheless, the first act is not strictly speaking illegal.

If this gives the public choice student a rather cool attitude towards political enthusiasms associated with particular candidates, his attitude towards the professional bureaucracy is equally cool but technically more complex. The view that the individual bureaucrat is not attempting to maximise the 'public interest' very vigorously but is attempting to maximise his own utility just as vigorously as you and I has been held for a very long time by most people in the backs of their minds. But bringing it into formal theory is a public choice accomplishment. So far this revelation has not had much impact on any real world government, but policy implications are regularly drawn from it by public choice students. One particular conclusion is the feeling that it is undesirable to have monopolistic government bureaus. Since almost all previous discussion of government efficiency had been dominated by a desire to eliminate 'duplication', the change is very radical indeed.

Contracting Out
The desire that there be a number of government bureaus whose performance can be compared by the legislative body is a new theme in policy which has emerged from public choice. Subordinate to this theme are two more radical variants. The first is the suggestion that many government activities can be contracted out instead of run by government agencies. This would be particularly easy if we did not have a monopoly structure and the government agency were broken up into a number of small units and contracted out unit by unit. Thus, we would not contract out the Navy, but we might contract out individual aircraft carriers. By this line of reasoning, it would not be of immense importance whether the holder of the contract for the USS Enterprise was the West Point Alumni Association or the US Postal Service. As long as they had to bid competitively, they would be under pressure. Of course, it would be important that the holder of the contract on the USS Enterprise did not have contracts on all the other naval vessels.

This proposal is not so radical in application as it is in theory, since governments already contract out various services. In the United States, highways are normally built by contracting out and then maintained by collective bureaucratic organisations. There seems no reason for the distinction. Similarly, for many years the Air Force purchased all its ordnance, whereas the Army and the Navy manufactured their own. Again, there seems no reason for the distinction. The most complicated and technically difficult parts of military activity seem to be contracted out, whilst routine activities are retained for direct government control.[13]

Most public choice students would be more radical in their proposals for contracting out and, in particular, would favour competition, whether from separate government agencies or separate private companies. However, though a competitive market works better than a non-competitive market, if the people purchasing the goods are government bureaucrats, it may not work particularly well. The US military external procurement industry is, I believe, massively more efficient than what remains of the direct military production of its own material. Unfortunately, this is not saying a great deal. Large-scale inefficiencies remain, probably because the purchasing agencies are bureaucracies sheltered against duplication and with an incentive structure such that for any given purchasing agent, the more money he spends the better off he is.

Summary

To sum up, the difference between a public choice student and a non-student of this relatively new discipline in policy matters is very largely a difference in attitude which arises from his knowledge of public choice. Much traditional reasoning has turned on totally unrealistic ideas about the efficiency of government. The student of public choice will not think that government is systematically engaged in maximising the public interest, but assumes that its officials are attempting to maximise their own private interests. In this, of course, they are like managers of, for example, United States Steel. The public choice student will feel that both in the private

---

[13] The famous U-2 was piloted by an employee of Lockheed Aircraft, not by an Air Force officer. For a long period our early-warning network in the far north was a subsidiary of the American Telephone and Telegraph Company, with only a very few military officers compelled to live in these frigid and unpleasant surroundings for supervisory purposes.

market and in the government sector there are institutions which tend to lead individuals maximising their own interests to, at least to some extent, provide goods for other people as a byproduct. In neither case is the institutional structure so designed that perfection is obtained. Unfortunately, much previous analysis has implicitly assumed that perfection was obtained in the government sector. The public choice student knows that it is not, and that insight affects his policy views. He is also aware of a number of possible improvements in the structure of government. Thus, his ideas of policy are apt to be different both in the fact that he is less enthusiastic about government and that among the policy considerations he is willing to consider (and may be devoted to) are structural changes in government.

2

VOTING PARADOXES

MOST MODERN DEMOCRACIES ARE REPRESENTATIVE GOVERNMENTS – that is, most decisions which are not made inside the bureaucracy are made by elected representatives. Most democracies in the world use a procedure called 'proportional representation' or the 'single member constituency'.[1] Before assessing the advantages and disadvantages of these techniques, let us consider the following.

Government of the Roman Republic

The Roman Republic, everyone will admit, was very successful. However, it practised a rather peculiar method of making a number of important decisions. Called consulting the 'auspices', it involved the examination of a freshly slaughtered ox by a 'specialist' in order to determine whether the ox's liver was 'auspicious'. Another method used by the Romans was to see whether a group of chickens ate freely or simply looked unhappy. There is an amusing incident connected with the First Punic War. A Roman admiral offered some food to the chickens on the deck of his flagship and presumably because they were seasick, they did not eat. He then said: 'If they won't eat then let us see if they will drink.' With that he threw them into the sea, and went into battle. It turned out the chickens knew more than he did.

In spite of this peculiar method of making decisions, the Romans were by all accounts an extremely successful nation. It may be that the improvement in morale in the troops as a result of consulting the auspices, made up for the randomness of the outcome. It will surprise

---

[1] There are different types of proportional representation. The 'Hare' method is used (though very little) almost exclusively in English-speaking countries. The other is used in most non-English-speaking democracies.

most readers that much the same criticism of randomness can be made about the use of voting to make collective decisions in a democracy. There is a mathematical proof, around for almost 50 years, showing that voting is subject to paradoxes and may indeed generate random outcomes.

Voting Paradoxes

Let us consider the following simple example in which three people, Mr One, Mr Two, and Mr Three, are choosing between three alternatives (A, B, and C). Each of them has preferences for the three as shown in Figure 1.

Figure 1		
Mr 1	**Mr 2**	**Mr 3**
A	B	C
B	C	A
C	A	B

Using simple majority voting in which the alternative with the most votes wins, we put A against B and then put the winner, which in this case would be A, against the remaining alternative, C. In this case C would win. But suppose we had started out differently. Instead, suppose we had put B against C, in which event B would win, and then B against A, in which event A would win. Or finally, suppose we had put C against A, in which event C would win, and then C against B with a win for B. The voting paradox is that any one of the three outcomes can be reached by a simple majority voting procedure, depending on the order in which the alternatives are considered.

What can we do about this? First, if we have a person who determines the order in which the three alternatives are voted upon, he can 'rig' the agenda so that whichever alternative he prefers wins regardless of the views of the others. If, however, we permit people to vote on the order of voting, we would simply reproduce the same paradoxical situation that we have shown above.

This paradox, or another one, will be encountered in voting, no matter what voting procedure is used. There are two problems with which we must deal. One is that we do not really know how often people's preferences will result in this paradox. In the case of few alternatives, there probably are not many of these problems, but in the real world, because there are always many alternatives, the likelihood of a paradox is greatly increased. The large number of alternatives is concealed from the average observer because the voting process usually winnows them down.

In the United States, for example, there are literally hundreds of politicians who think about becoming president. The bulk of them give it up with only minor exploration of their political opportunity set. A considerable number, however, go through the primary process which winnows the aspirants to two (or three, as in the 1992 and 1996 presidential elections), and then there is a choice between the finalists. In this case, the paradox occurs over the entire process, not simply in the final decision between the two potential candidates.

Condorcet (1743–1794), one of the people who discovered the paradox discussed above, suggested that we should choose the alternative which can get a majority against each of the others in simple pairwise voting. Unfortunately, there frequently is no such choice, as in the example given above, but in Britain there normally is.

The British Electoral System and the Paradox

The British electoral system illustrates the paradox. The Liberal Democrat Party would probably beat either the Conservative or Labour parties in a series of two-party elections because the Conservatives would prefer the Liberals to Labour and the Labour voters would prefer the Liberals to the Conservatives. The only party which has a reasonably strong chance of winning the support of the majority of the populace in a set of two-party contests is reduced to extreme weakness by the voting method used. However, what you think of this analysis will depend on your view of the Liberal Democrat Party.

Much research has been done about the likelihood that the paradox will occur with any given voting system but it has not provided reliable results. The opinion of this author, having read most of the research and contributed some of it, is that paradoxes are probably very common, but they most likely cover only a restricted portion of the available alternatives. Out of 10 alternatives, only three would be likely to win, but the choice among those three would be either random or determined by the order of voting. But this is just my opinion; no one who is familiar with the literature can feel really confident about a right answer.

Proportional Representation

Furthermore, the above argument assumes we are using only one method of voting. A very large number of different voting systems is in use around the world. The two most common methods of voting are proportional representation on the Continent and single-member constituencies in Britain and some English-speaking countries (Australia and Ireland are the exceptions). There is an important difference between the English-speaking system of single-member constituencies and systems based on proportional representation which aim at permitting substantially every sizeable group in a society to have direct representatives in the legislature.

For simplicity, let us consider the method of proportional representation used in the Netherlands and in Israel in which the whole legislature is selected from one big national area. The parties nominate a considerable number of candidates. Individual voters simply tick the party they favour. The seats are then divided among the parties according to the number of people who have selected particular parties. Thus even with a tiny part of the population behind him, a candidate can nevertheless sit in the legislature because that portion of the population which backs him is more than the minimum number required to put a single person in the legislature. In the US the representation of very small groups is unlikely to happen.[2]

In the proportional representation system, the individual party is apt to represent a rather tight collection of special interests: these parties then make up coalitions in the legislature for the purpose of passing specific bills. In the single-member constituency system, the coalition between various interests is, in essence, made up by an individual legislator in his constituency. Obviously, different legislators have different collections of interests behind them and these affect the coalitions they make in the legislature. It remains

---

[2] Under the US system a small minority which is geographically concentrated may get a representative in Congress. In the 1930s and early 1940s, there was a Communist who represented an atypical district in Congress.

true, however, that more of the coalition building in the English-speaking system is done in the electoral districts and less in Parliament than is true in the countries which use proportional representation.

Single-Member Constituencies

The single-member constituency is currently the standard form in most English-speaking countries.[3] Under this system, the population is divided geographically into single constituencies. Usually the constituencies have about the same number of voters in each of them. Sometimes, however, this is not true: the US Senate is an obvious example. The people who hold the seats in these constituencies are mostly elected by one of two systems. The first, used in Britain and most of its former colonies, is 'first-past-the-post'. Under this system, a large number of candidates may be nominated for a given office and the one with the largest number of votes is declared elected regardless of how few those votes may be. In present day Britain, for example, the party in power normally receives less than the majority of the votes because there are three major parties. Allende in Chile became president with only 36 per cent of the vote because his two opponents split the remainder of the vote almost evenly between them. It is sometimes said that 'first-past-the-post' leads to a government with strong parties because splinter parties have almost no chance of putting anyone in the legislature. Although there is a strong drive in 'first-past-the-post' systems to form large coalitions in order to win, this drive is not overwhelming and sometimes may fail.

With proportional representation, Britain would normally have a coalition government, usually composed of the Liberals and one other party, since a coalition of the Labour Party and the Conservative Party would be unlikely. It is likely that the Prime Minister would normally be Liberal. Exactly how large the Liberal vote would be is hard to say since the current polls are based on the opinions of people who are accustomed to the present method and

---

[3] It is also the standard form in India and there are more citizens in India than in all of the English-speaking countries combined. India adopted the system while it was part of the British Empire.

have not thought about how they would operate under the other system. That proportional representation would greatly change the outcome is fairly obvious.

The Variety of Voting Rules

Many different voting rules are used in the world and each leads to a somewhat different outcome. Saari has produced a rigorous mathematical proof that for a given set of voters with unchanged preferences, any outcome can be obtained by at least one voting method.[4] The reader should now understand why our system may have some resemblance to that used by the Roman Republic. We have been quite successful, but so were the Romans. Democracy in the modern world has not lasted as long as the Roman Republic, however. Let us hope we do not find our Caesar.

It is hoped that the above discussion will have convinced the reader there are relatively few strong, positive arguments for democracy. The basic argument in its favour is that the known alternatives seem to be much worse. Any form of government is apt to perform in a manner which is far from ideal. This is true of democracy, but democracy is not as far from ideal as is a dictatorship. We have discussed the strongest criticisms one can make against democracy but in the formal work by public choice scholars there are two more encouraging findings. One is the median preference theorem, which is explained below. The other is logrolling which is the subject of Chapter 3.

The Median Preference Theorem

Three voters with the same preferences as Figure 1 are shown in a different way in Figure 2. The alternatives are arranged on the horizontal axis and each voter is represented by a line whose height represents his comparative evaluation of the different alternatives.

---

[4] D. G. Saari, 'Millions of election outcomes from a single profile', in *Social Choice and Welfare*, Vol. 9 No. 4, 1992, pp. 277–306. My discussion has been made readable to the non-technical reader by using only simple proofs. Let me frankly admit that I do not fully understand Saari's proof. I will assume that, based on his reputation and that of his colleagues, his analysis is correct.

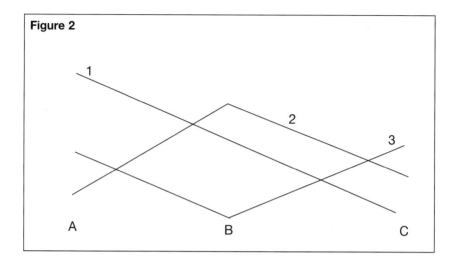

Figure 2

I should say that the exact shapes of these lines are of little importance. Their relative height is all we need for the analysis at this point.

If the reader wishes to experiment, it is obvious that if the preferences are in the shape as drawn, there is exactly the same paradox as found in Figure 1. The preference lines for the three voters are drawn for another three alternatives in Figure 3. Note that,

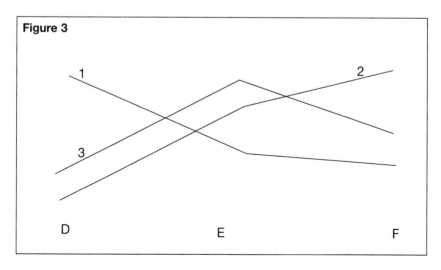

Figure 3

in this case, there is no paradox. The alternative in the middle can beat either of the other two.

E is called the median preference and there is, indeed, a median preference theorem. If it is possible to arrange the alternatives on the horizontal axis in such a way that the individuals have a single peak and in each case their preferences decline monotonically as we move away from the peak, then the median preference applies and the paradox we discussed does not occur.

The median preference theorem is quite simple. Assuming that the candidates of two parties are intent on winning the election, and assuming that voters will vote for that candidate who most closely approximates their own preferred political position, politicians will not choose political positions out on the wings of the distribution. If a candidate takes a political position in the wings on the voter distribution, he can be beaten at the polls by a candidate who moves into the middle of the distribution of preferences. To avoid losing the election, both candidates in a two-party election are induced to take middle-of-the-road political positions. The smart politician will choose a position near the middle of the distribution in order to avoid being outmanoeuvred by his opposition and losing the election. The opposing candidate must also go to the middle because otherwise he will lose the election. In short, in order to contemplate victory or to avoid being beaten, both parties will tend to choose political positions which are close to one another and in the middle of the distribution.

Median Preference and the Stability of Equilibrium

At first glance it might seem unlikely that this kind of arrangement would be common. Nevertheless, empirical work has shown that something like it occurs. The obvious case is the left to right continuum which may be used to describe the ordinary person's view of politics in which the unhappiness of voters is in proportion to the distance from their ideal point to the government's policies. This median preference phenomenon results in a stable equilibrium.

It is true that many people may not like the implication of this equilibrium that the median preference is apt to be 'mediocre'. It does, however, offer more than stability in that if the preferences are arranged in this way, choosing the median preference means that the sum of the dissatisfaction among all voters will be minimised. Proving this requires some special assumptions, but they are not particularly unreasonable.

The Many Dimensions of Politics

Politics, however, is not a single dimensional phenomenon. The farmers, for example, are primarily interested in the size of the subsidies made available to them, whether they come from the right or from the left of the political spectrum. The farmers of Iowa, to provide just one example, are generally thought to be on the far right politically. In 1964, they voted against Barry Goldwater, the candidate from the right, because of his opposition to farm subsidies. This was probably the only issue on which they agreed with his opponent, Lyndon Johnson. When Goldwater lost by a very wide margin in 1964 to Johnson, the party made a deliberate effort to pick a more moderate candidate in the 1968 election. After George McGovern (considered too liberal) was trounced by Nixon in 1972, the Democrats selected the more moderate Jimmy Carter in 1976.

Something similar happened to Ronald Reagan in 1976 when he was denied the Republication presidential nomination, to a very large extent due to his opposition to farm subsidies. In 1980, having learned his political lesson, he said that he did not understand the farm problem. He has, so far as I know, never endorsed the farm subsidies.

If the voters tend to be interested in different subjects, we get a more complicated form which goes beyond the limitations of two-dimensional diagrams and has to be dealt with by Cartesian algebra. Mathematically, this is not an insuperable problem but we can simplify it by thinking in only two dimensions. Let us suppose that we are voting solely on the size of the appropriations for the army and navy. In Figure 4, we put the army appropriation on the vertical axis and the navy on the horizontal axis with the ideal points of eight voters shown by the letters A–H, respectively.

Each voter's satisfaction would decline as he or she moved away from the letter representing his or her preferences. Duncan Black (1908–1991) discovered a very simple proof that in this type of

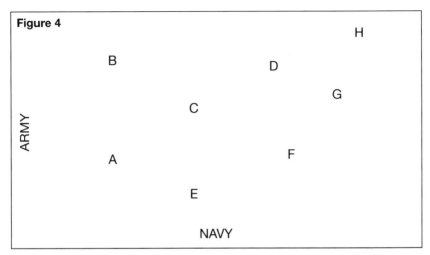

Figure 4

situation there normally would be no equilibrium. However, democratic politics usually involves parties, and parties to some extent solve this problem. Parties create a bundle of policies intended to attract the maximum number of voters. If there are two parties, it can be shown that they will end up near the centre of the 'cloud of voter preferences'. Figure 5 includes a line which is intended to divide the optimum points, with one party on one side and the other on the other side.

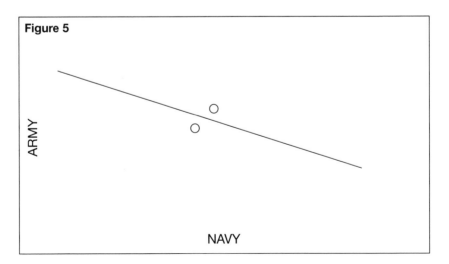

Figure 5

Coalitions and Convergence

This is to be expected in democratic voting in a two-party system. What we would expect in a proportional representation system is a multi-party system. The policies of the parties will not converge in the centre, but the policies of the coalitions which they put together in order to produce a government will converge in this way.[5]

The British situation is peculiar because the Liberal Party is, in essence, between the Conservative and Labour parties. Therefore, it is unnecessary for either party to get a majority of the votes in order to win; around 45 per cent is adequate in most cases. This means that the pressure for the two parties to come very close together in their policies is much weaker in Britain than in most countries. There is more difference between the Labour and Conservative parties than there is between the Republican and Democratic parties in the US.

Moral Principles and Politics

It will be noted that in this discussion, which is a relatively objective summary of the existing literature, nothing has been said about 'good' policies or the 'right' way to govern. The reason for this omission is they do not seem to affect government, except insofar as the voters themselves favour such policies. Do the voters, as they have in the past, turn against slavery or against segregation on essentially moral grounds? If they do, policies will be selected for moral reasons. From the politician's standpoint, however, this is not much different from such matters as the location of a dam in a constituent's region. In both cases, in order to win the election, it is essential for the politician to determine what the voters want and then offer it to them.

As stated earlier in this chapter, politicians, like the voters themselves, are sometimes driven by moral principles, but mainly, like you and me, they are interested in their own well-being. They are willing to make some sacrifices (lose a few constituents or interest-group support) for moral principle, to help the poor, or for some

---

[5] If you only have a few voters, seven to 10, the median preference theorem is weak. For voters in the millions, however, it dominates.

other desirable social goal, but the amount they are willing to sacrifice is not very large. We normally conceal that from ourselves by talking a great deal about moral issues, but if you observe how people behave, they normally give 5 per cent or less of their wealth to helping others for moral reasons.

The so-called 'median preference' theorem turns out to have an immense practical value in making formal empirical tests of various political problems. It has been used more than any other single mathematical approach. Nevertheless, in the real world, it is only an approximation. Logrolling, which is discussed next, is both more important and more realistic.

3

LOGROLLING

'LOGROLLING' IS AN UNUSUAL WORD BUT ITS MEANING IS SIMPLE: logrolling is vote trading. One member of Parliament or Congress, for example, will agree to vote for legislation [a bill] that another member wants in return for his or her vote on another issue. Logrolling is a very common phenomenon in any democratic political system. Indeed, in most democracies it dominates the political selection process, although it is frequently concealed from public view. Or its form is disguised in order to make it more palatable to members of the public with moral precepts against such 'political market activities'.

Anyone familiar with law-making knows that legislators frequently vote for legislation they really do not like in return for another legislator's agreement to vote for something they favour strongly. Vote trading is much more open in the American legislature than in Europe, although it certainly occurs everywhere. Perhaps because it is more open in the United States, the Americanism 'logrolling' is used to refer to this economic dimension of the public sector decision-making apparatus.

Logrolling is known by all students of politics, but until the development of public choice as a discipline it tended to receive little attention. Political scientists who did talk about vote trading viewed it realistically, but they also rarely had much to say and there was general moral disapproval of the phenomenon.

The Concept of Logrolling

Ordinary people in Europe or Britain frequently do not realise that their governments engage in this kind of activity. As it happens I know one of the more intellectual members of the British Parliament, who was sufficiently successful in politics to be made a cabinet minister. One evening I privately asked if it was true that British MPs would on occasion agree to vote for a bill or law which they really did not support in return for some one else voting for a measure they favoured strongly. While this kind of exchange of political support is quite open in the US, in Britain I thought it was simply concealed. My question evoked an immediate and vigorous denial.

On the following day in a prepared speech to a large audience, he explained how Parliament operated. He said: '[Y]ou go to committee meetings where you simply don't care about the outcome and vote in accordance with a colleague. You then take him to your committee, and when they vote, you hold up his hand.' Obviously, since he denied it privately, and explained it in detail in public, he simply did not fully understand the situation. He was shocked at a formal discussion of a trade in votes, but he was so accustomed to doing it that he was willing to say that he did it, as long as vote trading was not put in these general terms. When I called the contradiction to his attention, perhaps because he is an intellectual type, he immediately agreed that his private remarks were false.

Explicit and Implicit Logrolling

Logrolling is usually classified as either explicit or implicit. Explicit logrolling refers to situations in which there is a clearly defined trade of votes by two politicians. In the US Congress logrolling is fairly open and above board. While it is true that the bulk of the negotiations take place in committee sessions, cloakrooms, and congressional offices, there is no particular secret as to what is actually going on. People realise that the art of legislation involves bargaining, haggling, and efforts made to sweeten deals.

As an example of logrolling, let us consider the interstate highway system in the US. Because the system was financed by a tax on the gasoline consumed by all drivers – those who drive on the interstate highways and those who do not – any given community can be better off if it has one of the interstates running through it, but it must also pay for other interstates built in other parts of the country. Although one would expect that Arizona would want an internal interstate, and to some extent other interstates; generally speaking, her citizens would not favour being taxed in order to build interstates in Florida. During his period of office, President Eisenhower used implicit logrolling rather than explicit logrolling to resolve this problem. He simply 'packaged' the interstate proposals so that they benefitted a majority of state constituencies. The individual member of Congress, instead of having to develop his own bargains with other members, could simply look at the whole collection and decide whether he would vote for it or not. This does not eliminate logrolling, but rather obscures it. In the same way, political candidates try to get elected through developing 'packages' in the form of platforms and positions on particular issues.

Explicit logrolling is more visible, but at the same time more complicated to develop. Suppose that the congressional delegation from one state (Texas) is interested in having a large publicly funded project like the 'Supercollider' in their state. It goes to the delegations from other states and offers to support projects they desire in exchange for supporting Texas to get the Supercollider. For example, Texas may approach New York to support urban renewal projects of benefit to cities, or states such as Oregon or Louisiana to support flood control programmes of benefit to them. Note there is no reason in this type of logrolling why the coalition that votes for the Supercollider in Texas should be the same coalition of states as that which votes for the urban renewal or flood control programmes.

Implicit logrolling is more complex and can be implied from the way the legislation is proposed. For instance, measures which different politicians favour can simply be incorporated in one piece of legislation and a single vote taken on the bundle. Regardless of whether it is explicit or implicit, logrolling occurs because most laws have differential effects on groups and parts of the country. In short, any legislation is likely to affect some people more than others. Changes in tax laws are a very good example of legislation which will benefit some citizens more than others.

Benefits and Harm from Logrolling
Nor is logrolling undesirable in all cases. For example, suppose there is a project which will benefit some city, say Tucson, very greatly and which would have a relatively modest cost to the national taxpayer. While the total benefit received by the people in Tucson may exceed the cost of the project, if it were paid for by a national tax, the

proposal for government to fund the project would most assuredly be lost in the absence of logrolling.

If logrolling can clearly create benefits for the society, it can also cause harm. Consider a very simple society of five people, Mr. A, Mr. B, Mr. C, Mr. D, and Mr. E. Further, assume that each represents another constituency: 1, 2, 3, 4, and 5. Suppose this legislature, shown in Figure 6, can vote for individual projects, and the costs will be spread across all five constituencies. The size and number of constituencies is a simplification over the actual situations which are likely to occur, but not too much. The use of only five voters is a radical simplification and the particular phenomenon described probably would not work with only five voters. It requires more voters, but it is a good deal more difficult to put in the form of a diagram if we use 435 voters as found in the US House of Representatives. For this reason, we will continue the five voters example. Assume there are a number of projects, each of which will provide a benefit of $10.00 for one constituency, and each of which costs $5.00. This means that a tax of $1 will be imposed on each constituency so the net gain for the beneficiary constituency will be $9.00. Figure 6 shows the gain or loss to each constituency from each of these five bills. The reader will note that four of the constituencies always lose on each bill, and hence at first glance we might expect that none of the bills will pass.

Then comes logrolling. Suppose that Mr. A makes a deal with Mr. B and Mr. C, under which he agrees to vote for the expenditure in their constituency if they vote for the one in his. His bill thus gets a majority vote, and passes. Mr. B, already having Mr. A's vote, makes a deal with Mr. D to get his vote in return for agreeing to vote for Mr. D, and project 2 passes. Mr. C, once again, having Mr. A's vote makes a deal with Mr. E, of a similar nature, and project 3 passes. Mr. D and Mr. E , each of whom already have one vote, make a deal with each other and projects 4 and 5 pass. As a result the society as a whole is better off with this set of bargaining.

So far, logrolling appears to have worked very well. Unfortunately, there is an intermediate class of issues where logrolling works to the detriment of society. Suppose that the benefit of these projects was only $3.01. The same set of bargains could be

Figure 6

	A	B	C	D	E
1	9	-1	-1	-1	-1
2	-1	9	-1	-1	-1
BILLS 3	-1	-1	9	-1	-1
4	-1	-1	-1	9	-1
5	-1	-1	-1	-1	9

CONSTITUENCY

gone through, but society would be markedly worse off as a result of the passage of this particular collection of bills. Consider that the return to voter A of a bill (which costs $1.00 to each of the five taxpayers) is $3.01. He would be willing to trade a favourable vote on two other issues for two votes on his issue. This would net him $0.01 on the entire deal while the society pays $5.00 for a project worth only $3.01. In these cases, logrolling reduces the efficiency of government.

We should also briefly point out another possible outcome of logrolling. With such a small group as five voters, there is some probability that three of them, say Mr. A, Mr. B, and Mr. C, could enter a permanent arrangement under which they voted for projects that benefited the three exclusively and against projects that benefited Mr. D and Mr. E. With this arrangement they have greater gains over time. It is not obvious that socially this is any better than the full logrolling solution, but it would benefit the people who made the bargain.

The problem with such a bargain is that it is unstable with large numbers of voters. Mr. C, for example, having voted through the projects for Mr. A and Mr. B, might then be approached by Mr. D and Mr. E, to offer him a very good deal on another project which will benefit his district many times over its cost. Once again, with only five voters, one might argue that Mr. C would not go along with it. However, with a large number of voters this is apparently what happens. The result is that all of the projects go through, including those whose net value to society is negative.

Thus logrolling partly explains such public sector programmes as agricultural subsidies. In practice, the situation as discussed in

Chapter 2 on voting is likely to be worse. Assuming that the voter is very badly informed, one could readily anticipate a large random component of further errors. Unfortunately, it is even worse than that since voters are normally particularly badly informed about legislation which affects them very little. Aside from such possible economic inefficiency (see Chapter 4), there might be other objections to logrolling.

The Morality of Logrolling

Some people regard vote trading as immoral. Indeed, it is sometimes prohibited, ineffectively by law. Duncan Black, one of the founders of public choice, was particularly vigorous in this regard. I have heard of many other people who have similar views. Perhaps they, like the MP mentioned above, would admit their error once it was brought to their attention. As will be explained, a simple, rather minor change in procedure makes vote trading once again moral in the minds of some practitioners and observers. I do not understand the distinction, but I also observe that other people think it important.

Let us take the simple type of logrolling with simple direct trades. Congressman Morris Udall (Democrat-Arizona) who for many years wanted the Central Arizona Project, made trades ('swaps') with a number of legislators. Interestingly enough, he included among his trading partners a number of environmentalists who wanted to prevent natural resource development in Alaska, a state known for its pristine wilderness. In return for his opposition to various projects in Alaska, the environmentals voted for the immensely wasteful Central Arizona Project.[1] Of course, Mr Udall had to make other trades in order to get his 'pork', but he was an experienced congressman and fully accustomed to the realities of politics. The trades required that other legislators vote contrary to their preferences on individual items. It is this distortion of 'true preferences', rather than legislators engaging in vote trading, which

---

[1] The Central Arizona Project is complicated and the reader need know nothing about it except that it was wasteful as well as environmentally damaging.

many consider immoral. Simply stated, the legislator's public behaviour does not square with his private values.

Some politicians consider it is possible to make logrolling moral by 'bundling' all these projects together in one gigantic bill. Although the legislator may object to many individual parts of the bill, the provisions that he favours are assumed to counterbalance any negatives he may hold for parts of the bill. In looking at the bill as a whole, the legislator can 'honestly' say he favours it.

The view that this form of logrolling is moral ignores the procedure by which the bundling takes place. The trades take place in committee where members may vote against their preferences in some items in order to get others passed, with the final outcome becoming one big bill. Indeed, Congressman Udall made his trades in committee and the Central Arizona Project was included as part of a very large bill. Nevertheless, there are other politicians who regard this vote trading in committee as morally correct, whereas direct trading of votes in the open forum of the legislature is thought to be immoral.

In this context, the 'moral' distinction seems misplaced. After all, if the benefits from the Central Arizona Project had been greater than the cost, it would have been desirable. But, if the taxes fell on the USA as a whole, this would have been opposed by congressmen from outside Arizona. Arrangements (inducements) for these representatives to get some compensating 'pork' for their district were neither immoral nor unwise. This type of trade is dealt with in economics without difficulty. A special tax on the beneficiaries would have been ideal, but it would be unconstitutional.

Consummation of Trades
Unfortunately, the situation we describe is not as simple as that. In the first place, you need to obtain the support of a majority of only one in the legislature in order to consummate one of these bargains. Thus you need a pay-off for slightly more than half of the constituencies involved. However, in theory it is considerably more difficult because a constituency is represented by a person who has to carry a majority of his own constituents. Provided that the losses

are thinly distributed over the other regions, slightly more than a quarter of the total population has to benefit from the project.

Information Problems

Few congressmen calculate with such precision, but the information problems discussed earlier greatly exaggerate the waste. Most people are not as well informed about their vote as they are about purchasing items for personal consumption. Indeed, even well-informed people normally do not know a great deal about the details of the political setting. Consider, for example, the office of 'constable', an elective office in Arizona. I am sure that many share my ignorance of the constable's duties. The extent of knowledge about most people running for the office is probably limited to the name of the candidate. Serious investigation of exactly what the constable does and the relative capacities of the candidates for the job is not a cost-effective use of an individual's time since their one vote out of the 100,000 voters involved would not be likely to change the outcome of the election. Similar reasoning applies, I am sure, to all readers of this *Primer*. Public opinion polls have established that the average American cannot, except near the time of the election, tell you the name of his Congressman. It should also be noted here that if you provide the Congressman's name the average American will say 'Oh, yes, I remember now, he is my Congressman.'

Apparently most people feel they are moderately well informed in politics because there are some subjects that interest them. While their understanding of contemporary issues may not be accurate or detailed, it may seem satisfactory to them. Cases in which people do gather information tend to be those that affect an individual specifically. Consider the following examples: a proposal to establish or remove a tariff on a product you manufacture; a proposal for a large public works project in your immediate vicinity; and, finally, as in Tucson, closing a military facility which provides a large payroll for the region. Obviously, such programmes with their particularised and easily understandable effects are more likely to be known to those most closely affected than to the average voter. Other voters will, of course, be expected to know about the proposals which affect them.

It is not only access to the information which is important, but whether the information will influence your vote in the next election. By the time of the next election, the Congressman knows that many people, even those who write to him, will have forgotten about the matter or come to regard it as less important than other issues.

Congressmen sometimes claim in their speeches that they did not know that a specific provision was in a bill they supported. In many cases they are, no doubt, perfectly honest in saying this. The bills passed by the US Congress are so numerous and lengthy that it would be physically impossible for every Congressman to read every bill in its entirety. Frequently, the bill is changed at the last minute and the final text is not available for all Congressmen until after the vote. However, anyone who reads the text of laws passed by the US Congress in a given session immediately discovers a large number of concerns of which he is ignorant. The concerns which voters hold intensely are far more important to the Congressman than those about which they have only minor feelings and certainly more important than those of which they are not aware.

In Britain the situation is not as bad because the number of bills passed is much lower. On the other hand, as in the US, many activities are undertaken by the government which would arouse dissent and, perhaps, severe pressure from the House of Commons if they were better known. In almost all of these cases, there is a small minority which feels strongly about the matter, and a large majority which knows little about it. In cases where there are opposing minorities, there is apt to be a good deal of dispute brought to public attention.

Most political battles are likely to take place over proposals which are of primary interest to small groups. Congressmen wishing to be re-elected will take careful account of issues and bills which strongly affect small minorities, whether it is a reduction of transfers to them, an increase in the taxes specific to them (like road taxes for freight carriers), or a special tax exemption. Considerably less attention is given to the issues affecting the general population because the voters are unlikely to be strongly motivated to express their support or disfavour at the ballot box.

Organised Lobbying

The situation is more difficult because of the existence of organised lobbying and pressure groups. Once again, this is more visible in the United States than in the UK. While Britain has a smaller government and economy and the resources allocated to the special pleading of interest groups is presumably less, there is no reason to believe that it affects a smaller share of GDP in England than it does in the US.

In discussing the organisation of political pressure groups, the primary point is that it is, on the whole, unwise for me to invest a considerable amount of time or money pursuing activities that will have little effect on me personally. At the University of Arizona, many of my colleagues talk about political issues. Yet the issues which lead them to organise in order to bring pressure on the state government of Arizona or the federal government in Washington have direct effects on the university or on their working conditions.

This problem was formally analysed by Mancur Olson, who pointed out that when a relatively small number of people is heavily affected by a collective activity, it is in their interest to organise.[2] This occurs for several reasons. *First*, each individual in the group will either benefit a good deal if the political action is in his favour or be injured a good deal if it is against him. *Second*, since there are only a few of them, it is relatively easy (low transactions costs) for them to organise.

On the other hand, if the collective decision affects a large number of people but represents only a small amount to each of the group, the converse applies. Each of this large group would find only minor effects (either costs or benefits) from whatever is done. A large number of people experiencing a small loss is difficult to organise because each could reasonably think that his contribution to the joint lobby would make little difference in the likely success of the action. Hence, it is rational in such circumstances for the individual to avoid making his contribution.

---

[2] M. Olson, *The Logic of Collective Action*, Cambridge, Mass.: Harvard University Press, 1969.

Consider the following example. Suppose the proceeds of a tax of five pence levied on every citizen of Britain are to be given to the authors who have recently written learned pamphlets for the Institute of Economic Affairs. One would expect the authors would be very interested in this proposal, which, after all, for each author would be a lot of money. Hence, they would seek to bring pressure on the House of Commons to pass it.

Because the cost to the individual citizen is only five pence it would be foolish to allocate his resources to prevent it. Simply complaining to his MP might entail a greater burden than the loss of the five pence. In practice, of course, this tax to benefit Institute of Economic Affairs authors, although easy to understand, is not likely to be successful. While it is a simple transfer from a large number of voters to a few authors, the newspapers would, no doubt, create a public outcry which would prevent its adoption.

Concentrated Benefits and Diffuse Costs

On the other hand, laws or regulations which have this characteristic of diffuse costs and concentrated beneficiaries do sometimes become law. This may occur because the effect is disguised by superficially plausible propaganda or rationalisations developed by the pressure group. Consider the following example. At one time the US had a tariff to protect the manufacturers of the chin rests for violins. The total demand was such that there was only one company employing four or five people which made the chin rests. For violin purchasers who had to pay two or three cents more for the violin because of this tariff, the cost was much too small to lobby. Nevertheless, it was a worthwhile investment for the manufacturer of the small violin part to testify before the US Senate; no one testified on the side of the violin purchasers against the tariff.

The argument in defence of the tariff was the potential unemployment of the four or five engaged in manufacturing the chin rest. A tax, even a small tax, on violins to provide a pension for the employees of the company would have failed because, while economically more efficient, it would have been entirely too obvious.

As will be explained, the political aversion to simple direct transfers means that protected projects are much less efficient than they would be otherwise. The cost to the people who incur the cost is higher and the return to the people who receive the benefit is lower than it would be if a simple transfer was politically feasible.

Lobbying and Inefficient Transfers

The number of people involved in lobbying for such inefficient transfers is quite large in the US and in Britain. On the other hand, it is obvious that direct cash bribes are not used frequently since MPs and US Congressmen rarely retire immensely wealthy. When one considers the resources under their control, this shows they must be honest.

Contributions to individual politicians in the US and to political parties in Britain often receive a great deal of publicity from the news media. Such contributions influence the outcome of elections and laws, but it is easy to exaggerate their effect. For example, the US Congress has voted for itself large staffs, offices conveniently located in their home district, franking privileges (free postage), and so on. The value of these elaborate privileges to each Congressman is probably five or six times the campaign contributions he receives. To a large extent these perquisites of office are used to campaign for the Congressman's re-election and provide powerful protection for the incumbent.[3]

Interest groups are effective in bringing firmly to the attention of Congress that there are a number of voters whose strong views about a given issue will probably affect their votes in the next election. In addition, they may also provide a public interest camouflage by convincing Congressmen that their special legislation is in the public interest. Most of the people involved in this type of enterprise are highly intelligent, highly motivated and very persuasive; it is not

---

[3] It may very well be the case that Congress is willing to restrict campaign contributions because they have this money of their own. It is true that incumbents normally get larger contributions than their challengers. The opponents at least get some money whereas they do not have access to the perquisites of the incumbent.

surprising that they sometimes succeed in selling the Brooklyn Bridge to a Congressman or several Congressmen simultaneously.[4]

Lobbies and the 'Public Interest'

If you talk with an ordinary citizen who benefits from one of the special interest lobbies (such as the American Association of Retired People, environmental advocates, sugar producers, welfare recipients), he presents a series of public interest arguments with every appearance (which I am sure is genuine) of believing it. Nevertheless, it is the private interest argument which leads to the organisation of these groups, the transfer of funds, the protection of jobs and special privileges for special-interest groups. The public-interest arguments normally require that the project itself be designed in such a way that the direct transfer is hidden from the public eye. As an old example, in the US, depending on the weather, the farm programme costs some $20–30 billion each year. However, the real gain to the farmers is only $1 billion.[5] Indeed, some agricultural economists maintain that the farmers would, after a short period of confusion, be better off by the repeal of the whole programme.

Agricultural Protection

Current agricultural subsidies in the USA are an immensely inefficient transfer programme. We would be far better off with a direct tax on the people who buy bread with the money paid to the farmers than we are with the present system. Unfortunately, this obvious transfer would not become law because the transparency of the transfer would be considered scandalous by the average voter. Congressmen are fully aware of this and, in general, do not pass the type of bill that is obviously a direct transfer. This does not mean

---

[4] The selling of the Brooklyn Bridge is a comic story about the naïve people who are taken in by the fast-talking salesman who convinces them that a large and imposing structure can be purchased for a small amount of money.

[5] This relatively small amount is the result of restrictions which make it impossible for the farmers to use the most efficient techniques, but are part of the camouflage of the direct transfer.

transfers do not occur, but that indirect, devious methods of making them are adopted which are inefficient in the sense that the recipient receives less and the taxpayer pays more than if a direct transfer were used.

Abolishing Privileges

The result is that many projects bring benefits which are far less than their costs. As stated earlier in this chapter, this problem is not only characteristic of democracy. As anyone familiar with dictatorships realises, this problem occurs in a somewhat different and more unpleasant form in that type of government. The remedy for the problem is theoretically easy, but in practice quite difficult because it entails preventing the logrolling that leads to highly inefficient projects. The simplest way to accomplish this goal is to reduce the federal budget while making sure that the cuts fall predominantly on the projects of special-interest beneficiaries. Abolishing privileges would make everyone better off because, although almost everyone would lose some kind of special privilege, the cost of all of the special privileges held by others is greater than the benefit received from any one special privilege which an individual may have. The same is equally true of Britain and the US.

Concluding Comments

Unfortunately, there is a problem. Although I would gain from the abolition of these programmes, my gain would be greater if all of the special privileges were eliminated except those which benefited me specifically. Because this is true of all voters, the well-known prisoner's dilemma problem tends to mean that such reductions are rarely successful.[6] However difficult, it is not impossible. President Reagan's success in having a tax simplification bill passed through Congress reduced the basic tax rate of many people by eliminating special interest deductions. We can but hope that this will happen again in the future.

---

[6] The prisoner's dilemma is a situation in which two parties may gain from co-operation but they are not permitted to co-operate because of the institutional structure.

4

THE COST OF RENT SEEKING

IN RECENT YEARS, 'RENT SEEKING' HAS BEEN A MAJOR TOPIC IN PUBLIC CHOICE, and for that matter, economics in general. The term 'rent seeking' is now found in almost every issue of any economic journal. For a term that was invented only a rather short time ago, that is remarkable.[1] My personal definition is the use of resources for the purpose of obtaining rents for people where the rents themselves come from some activity which has negative social value. For example, if the US automobile industry invests resources in persuading government to impose a tariff on Korean cars, this makes the citizens of the country worse off. Hence, even though the automobile companies will gain, the investment of resources is rent seeking. The now burgeoning field of studies in rent seeking has been heavily concerned with government regulation of industry, although rents can be obtained in many other ways. Private monopolies, for example, are usually the result of rent-seeking activities. They are comparatively rare, but if this chapter were being written in 1890 the author might pay much more attention to J. P. Morgan and much less attention to the government. Another area of rent seeking is, of course, direct income transfers by the government in which Mr. A is taxed and Mr. B receives the money.

As one of the developers of the concept, I should say that I do not like the term 'rent seeking'. If I were to invest a large amount of resources in discovering a cure for cancer, I would, in the economic meaning of the term, be seeking a rent. The reader will agree, however, that our evaluation of this activity should be radically different from that of a pharmaceutical company which uses the Congress to

---

[1] The concept was invented in G. Tullock, 'The Welfare Costs of Tariffs, Monopolies and Theft', *Western Economic Journal*, Vol. 5, 1967, pp. 224–32. The phrase 'rent seeking' was coined in A.O. Krueger, 'The Political Economy of the Rent-Seeking Society', *American Economic Review*, Vol. 64, 1974, pp. 291–303.

ban a competitive product. One suspects that most economists when they use the phrase 'rent seeking' simply do not think of it as being closely connected with the kind of rent that one would obtain from my cancer cure. If someone is observed receiving a rent or, for that matter, engaging in activities which might lead to the rent, the first thought should be to inquire whether society as a whole is better off as a result of the activity/product which generates the rent.

Although rent seeking is essentially a new idea to modern scholars, and not explicitly discussed until the past 25 years, it would not have been much of a surprise to Adam Smith as he lived in the latter stages of a dying rent-seeking society. His work, in a real sense, gave the *coup de grace* to rent seeking. Whether, in the absence of Adam Smith, rent seeking would have survived and become important in England, or continued to die, is not clear. In any event, such ideas did spread. The 19th century was a period of little rent seeking in English-speaking countries. Thus, as economic thought developed, the mere prospect of using the government for the purpose of raising your income was decried, but not seriously analysed. The realisation that it could attract large amounts of resources was simply overlooked.

The Intellectual Origins of Rent Seeking

The concept of rent seeking as popularly perceived refers to such legal and illegal activities to obtain special privilege as seeking monopoly status, special zoning, quantitative restrictions on imports, protective tariffs, bribes, threats and smuggling. Until quite recently economists argued that government privileges, monopolies and so on were not very costly to society. According to the former orthodoxy, these factors involved transfers between the pressure group that got the monopoly profits and the customer who lost real income due to higher prices. Since they are both members of society, these transfers were thought to more or less cancel each other out. According to this view there would be only a very minor reduction in the total societal output even though the new monopoly was less efficient than competition.

With the higher price, some people who would have bought the product at the lower price did not do so, and hence, the 'consumer surplus' they would have obtained was simply gone. The consumer surplus of people who continued buying even at the higher price would be reduced, while the loss to them would be gained by the monopolist. Most people, of course, would have resented the transfer from the consumer to the monopolist, but from the standpoint of the whole society, there was no loss and hence only a redistribution to worry about. These studies, which had been accumulating for some time, measured the 'welfare triangle', which was thought to be the only cost. Most economists had been rather surprised by the small cost shown by the received doctrine.

It is now realised that this rather perverse line of reasoning is wrong. It assumes that the special privilege or monopoly is in essence a gift of God. In the real world, people have to work for special privilege. The logrolling discussed in Chapter 3 is one of the more important ways in which they compete for rents. However, there is no reason why resources invested in 'rent seeking' should have any higher return than if invested in other endeavours.

Consider a steel firm which faces competition from Japanese producers. The US steel producer has two alternatives. It can invest a lot of money in building state-of-the-art steel plants, and hence, meet the competition head-on. Or it can invest resources in lobbying to restrict the importation of Japanese steel. If the cost of getting that restriction was lower than the cost of building a new plant, they would never build new plants. Since we observe people building new plants, rather than going to Congress for restrictions on imports, it is obvious that the cost of the two investments must be fairly close, and indeed, the plant may be cheaper. Thus there must be a very large cost for getting the special privilege.

The Costs of Rent Seeking

These costs falls into several categories. First, there is literally the cost of the lobbying establishment. Anyone who has visited the capital city of a major industrial country – Washington, DC, would be a good example – immediately sees a very large rent-seeking industry. There are expensive restaurants where you can take Congressmen or high-ranking civil servants to dinner or for drinks. Other entertainment, of the less widely publicised sort, is often available. Aside from allowing lobbyists to deduct such entertainment as a cost of doing business, the US government subsidises the rent-seeking industry by maintaining such publicly funded entertainment as the Kennedy Center. Although it purports not to receive a government subsidy it does receive some such subsidies.[2] For the lobbyist, it is a relatively inexpensive place where Congressmen and others can be entertained.

Although in appearance such expenditures are quite sizeable, they represent a very small part of the social cost of rent seeking. The same is true of the campaign contributions which get a great deal of media attention. While the lobbying industry appears substantial in Washington or other major capital cities, it is really quite modest in comparison with the value of the privileges bestowed. The same would be true in London, although in such a very large city lobbying is not as conspicuous as in the US.

There are other costs of establishing special privileges. It is, to a considerable extent, a gamble. The industrial firm, the individual labour union, or the special-interest pressure group such as the Sierra Club, is in essence buying a lottery ticket when it decides to under-take lobbying activities to obtain a special privilege.[3] As for other types of lotteries, the winner makes a large profit, but the bulk of the people who buy lottery tickets lose and the total losses are larger than the benefit. One can organise a pressure group and lobby in Washington, but only hope for pay-back on your investment.

Yet the real cost of rent seeking comes from the distortion of the voting process. People in Arizona who voted for former Congressman Udall because he would get the Central Arizona Project through Congress normally did not know that Congressman Udall had supported a number of seemingly unrelated projects in

---

[2] Because it receives funding from the federal government, the salaries of its employees are set by the civil service scale.

[3] While the types of rents sought by the firm or union are fairly well known, many do not associate rent seeking with the activities of environmental organisations which seek laws to benefit their constituents or ensure their participation in the implementation and enforcement of environmental laws.

order to make this project a reality.[4] The cost to the Arizona voter of the Central Arizona project, if we count only his or her share of the taxes, is quite small. If we count the taxes the voter pays to support not only the Central Arizona Project but also all the other projects and bills that 'log-rolling' Congressman Udall voted for in order to get his project through, it would be very large (see Chapter 3).

Moreover, this total cost cannot be calculated because Congressmen do not publicly announce their trades in any detail. They will occasionally mention one and they will not conceal such 'log-rolling' trades. But taxpayers cannot expect them to provide a complete list of the trades necessary for the Central Arizona Project to become law. As a result of this absence of data, we can only guess the true cost. And the massive inefficiencies in our government sector, each of which benefits at least one group, is evidence that the total is at least as high as the direct benefits and probably much higher. The Central Arizona Project which produces only minor benefits to anyone is only one example. Others in the US include making Tulsa, Oklahoma, a deep water port and the construction of a canal which parallels the Mississippi which would hardly be a great benefit even to the citizens of Tulsa or the inhabitants of all the states along the canal.

A Short History of Rent Seeking

Most societies for which we have records have been rent seeking. It seems likely that the rapid progress in the last two centuries, as contrasted to the progress in previous centuries, is largely due to the departure of various governments from the rent-seeking society.[5] What clearly happened is that the rent-seeking society ended in Britain; and its great prosperity and in particular its military success

---

[4] Even for the citizens of Arizona, the Central Arizona Project was not a particularly good bargain. But they did not know that at the time.

[5] There is another quite relevant factor which is the invention of the patent system. See, for example, G. Tullock, *The Organization of Inquiry*, Durham, NC: Duke University Press, 1966, pp. 21–26.

led to a widespread emulation of British institutions. Napoleon III, Emperor of the French, was strongly in favour of free trade, probably because he spent much of his early life in Britain. It is not, of course, surprising that, granted its power and wealth, other countries rather unthinkingly might have copied Britain. Countries that escaped this influence, like most of South America, remained rent-seeking societies and continue to suffer from being poor and backward.

The rate at which rent seeking develops is controlled by many factors. The government may be so organised that rent seeking is complicated. A bi-cameral legislature, for example, makes rent seeking more expensive because decisions are more diffuse than in a legislature composed of one deliberative body. It follows that the additional expense will make rent seeking more expensive. As a consequence, there will be less of it. Similarly, if there are very frequent direct popular votes on bills, rent seeking is more difficult. The relatively small size of the Swiss government illustrates this effect. Lastly, any rule that complicates and makes the functioning of the government decision-making process less smooth will lower the amount of rent seeking.

Anyone looking at the history of the American state governments realises that they are avid rent seekers, continuously attempting to establish special privilege for various groups of their citizens. Their incomplete ability to exclude imports from other states, however, meant that these efforts largely cancelled out. The principal source of rent seeking today, the federal government, was largely inactive internally until the First World War.

For a considerable period I was an expert on China for the US Department of State. I was impressed that, during the period around 1750, there was no great difference in living standards and the general level of industrial and scientific progress in the Orient and in the West. Jesuit missionaries thought China had a higher level of civilization than Europe during the period prior to this. My experience in China and Korea had no direct conscious relevance to my later work in rent seeking, but perhaps this immersion in what were clearly rent-seeking societies may have, at the sub-conscious level, provided intellectual preparation for the idea of rent seeking.

China, like most of the rest of the world, had a society in which the principal way of getting ahead was to obtain a special privilege from the government. Essentially for accidental reasons, Western Europe, and in particular Britain, moved out of this type of society and turned to one where getting ahead depended upon production, not rent seeking. Watt invented the steam engine, and Edison the incandescent lamp. In China, on the other hand, equally talented people were engaged in seeking special privilege.

The steam engine and the electric light not only made their inventors wealthy, but also the rest of us far better off. The Chinese official who obtained the right to draw part of his income from one of the merchant houses that had a monopoly on foreign trade became equally wealthy, but he contributed nothing to the other people. Indeed, the results of his activities were to make them worse off.

Direct and Indirect Damage from Rent Seeking

There is no doubt that rent seeking in general leads to serious inefficiencies in this direct sense, but its indirect damage is even worse. Drawing the bulk of intelligent and energetic people in society into an activity which has no social product, or may have a negative social product, is more important in explaining the stagnation of these societies than the direct social cost of the rent seeking.

My own experience with lobbyists in Washington (which I might add has not been extensive), indicates they are very intelligent and energetic people with great charm, a necessary characteristic if they must deal with Congressmen and bureaucrats. They are the kind of people we would like to have driving forward in production. It should be noted that the objective of some lobbyists is to obtain a more open economy. Most, however, are on the other side – seeking special privilege. It is unfortunate that this collection of highly intelligent and energetic people who could make real contributions to society are reducing its efficiency.

Western countries are far from being dominated by rent seeking the way the Eastern countries were ruined. Indeed, a number of Eastern countries demonstrated that they could obtain high rates of growth by turning away from monopoly production and going instead into foreign trade. Taiwan has a group of traditional Chinese people who, if left to themselves, would have built a rent-seeking society. In order to survive, however, they had to export. Further, realising that their small government could not give them any special privileges in the US or Chilean market-places forced them to turn to efficient production as a means of obtaining markets. That is also true for Japan, South Korea, Hong Kong, and Singapore.

China, itself, after many generations under the old empire, which was probably the best governed of what might be called the traditional countries, has had a rather bad 20th century. The opening of the economy and the sharp curtailing of rent seeking by Deng Shiao Ping has converted it into the fastest growing country in the world. Even though there are signs of the revival of rent seeking, this unprecedented growth remains a remarkable feat.

But even if China is currently the fastest growing country in the world, this is from a low base, and obtaining a high percentage of improvement from a low base is quite easy. If you are only producing 10 tooth brushes a year, raising that to 20 represents a 100 per cent improvement. It is also true that their very large percentage increases still leave wages below levels which would be acceptable in Europe or the US. The sharp curtailment of the rent-seeking society in China is paying off richly. We can only hope that it continues.[6]

The Old, the Young and Rent Seeking

In general, Europe is moving towards the rent-seeking society, although in most cases, the individuals who become very wealthy by manipulating the government are outside the government rather than governmental officials. Many of the benefits obtained from rent seeking now are relatively small, and widely dispersed. In the US, the elderly are well organised and doing well in rent seeking: a large part

---

[6] We should keep in mind that historically many central Chinese governments have collapsed within 50 years or so from the time they were set up. These governments which have collapsed do not play an important role in history, which is dominated by the smaller sample of long-lasting dynasties. The average life expectancy of a new government in China is low. Whether the communists will be one of the dynasties like the Tang, which lasted a long time, or like Chin or Sui, which collapsed under their second emperor, we cannot say.

of the cost of maintaining their lobbying organisation is directly paid by the US government. Most of these people will tell you they are simply getting back the money they paid in earlier in the various programmes of the welfare state. They are getting back much more than their payments, however, and the cost is borne by the younger people who in turn are almost certain to get less back than they paid in.

The elderly are well organised, allied strongly with the welfare bureaucracy, and directly concerned with what in most cases constitutes a large part of their income. The younger people who pay are fooled as a result of Prince Bismarck's invention of a clever tax scheme under which they think they pay only half of the cost of the social security scheme. This, of course, is a more modern part of the rent-seeking society. There are a large number of people who can make use of their votes to obtain transfers, but on the whole they do not get very large amounts of money. The reduction in the total output of society has not been much, although it has led to diseconomies almost everywhere. It is clear that it will have detrimental long-run effects.

Conclusion

Prediction is a chancy business. The reader is free to make his or her prediction about the effects of rent seeking, and to disagree with the author. However, it should be kept in mind that there is also the steady growth of the total scope of bureaucratic control. This benefits the bureaucrats and not any one else. That the bureaucrats do not become vastly wealthy is no doubt an indication of their probity, but the costs to the community of rent seeking may still be gigantic.

I conclude by emphasising that at the present time we do not have adequate measures of rent-seeking costs. This deficiency occurs for reasons both theoretical and empirical. There is adequate theoretical basis for believing that rent-seeking costs are relatively high, and indeed for suspecting that many are hidden or disguised. They take many forms, including the failed bids, aborted enterprises, uncharted waste and threatened but never activated public policies. We know that most senior executives of large companies spend a fair amount of time in Washington. We also know that there has been a major relocation of trade associations away from commercial centres such as New York City to Washington, perhaps due to its cost advantages in securing special privilege.

5

BUREAUCRACY

BUREAUCRACY TRADITIONALLY HAS BEEN TREATED either as simply a 'bad word' or it has been assumed that the bureaucrat is concerned with maximising the public interest. Sometimes the same scholar has used both models simultaneously. Bureaucrats are much like other people and, like people in general, are more interested in their own well-being than in the public interest. The problem is to design an apparatus that leads bureaucrats in their own interest to serve the interests of the rest of us in the same way the baker is led by his own interest to serve the needs of the tailor.

British and American Bureaucracies

British and American government bureaucracies are, to some extent, different. This is partly because the American bureaucracy is much bigger and partly because the higher positions in the executive branch of the American government are generally held by political appointees and in Britain the career civil servants may attain very high positions. As a comparison, there are some 2,400 political appointees at the top levels of the US government. The political people at the head of the British bureaucracy are Members of Parliament and hence have to spend much time in Parliament, whereas in the US, except for the President himself, they are not directly connected with politics.

Another important difference is that the higher-level officials in the British government tend to maintain their positions for long periods of time, whereas most of the political appointees in Washington will have a relatively short tenure. They have interrupted their regular career to spend two or three years in Washington, either because they view such public service as a duty or because they expect to make contacts which will make them wealthier after they leave.

But there are many similarities between the US and Britain. The higher-level British bureaucrats will tell you that they simply carry out the instructions of their 'masters'. While this may be true, to some extent the relationship between the senior bureaucrats and the political heads of their departments is rather like the caricatures in the British television situation comedy, *Yes, Minister*. US political appointees, of course, will also tell you their role is to run a good government and to carry out the President's instructions. I do not doubt they are as sincere in their statements as their British counterparts.

Bureaucratic Interests
If these statements are true, however, the bureaucrats in both countries are most remarkable people. Most of us are more interested in ourselves and our family than we are in public sector duty although we will make some sacrifice of our own selfish interests to take a public sector job. Indeed, charitable contributions are made and occasionally we make decisions which are intended to help people outside our own family. But all this is, generally speaking, relatively minor compared to our interest in our own well-being.

In most bureaucracies the executive, whether in General Motors, the Department of State, or the Exchequer, is in a position where only to a minor extent is his own interest involved. Bureaucrats make many decisions which will have little or no direct effect on themselves and hence can be made with the best interests of General Motors or the American or the British people at heart. Unfortunately bureaucrats, in general, have only weak motives to consider these problems carefully, but they do have strong motives to improve their status in the bureaucracy, whether it is income, power, or simply the ability to take leisure while sitting in plush offices. They are likely to be more concerned with this second set of objectives than the first, although they may not put very much effort into it because not much effort is required.

Proposals for reorganising government in order to make bureaucracy work better remain at an early stage. Models based on the assumption that bureaucrats are attempting to maximise their own well-being rather than the public interest seem to have very considerable predictive value. Further, these models indicate – although as yet the full empirical evidence is not in – that the problem of bureaucracy is much more severe than was originally thought. Expansion of bureaucracies to the point where the entire social surplus from the service which they provide is absorbed in the pay of more and more bureaucrats seems to be an unavoidable outcome of the budget-maximising bureaucratic model.

Note that this demonstration that bureaucracies will, on balance, generate no public good is not dependent upon any assumption that the bureaucrats are idle or inefficient. It depends solely on the assumption that they are interested in maximising their own returns. In the real world, it would appear that bureaucrats are frequently inefficient, and hence the real-world situation may be worse than in the budget-maximising model of bureaucracy. It also appears likely that since bureaucrats can vote in a democracy, it has difficulty disciplining them. We would anticipate that the bureaucratic problems of democracies would be much worse than those of a despotism, although the problem could, of course, be solved if bureaucrats and their families were deprived of their vote as part of the conditions of employment (see below).

A great deal of this literature on bureaucracy (and, also, of that part of the economic literature which deals with government) not only assumes that such orders are meaningful and will be carried out; it also assumes that governments are in practice attempting to maximise the public interest. The observation that government will not 'maximise the public interest' simply because it is told to do so is not the same as the statement that corporations characteristically do not maximise profits. The latter statement means, in essence, that the corporations are not perfectly organised and therefore have an inbuilt structural error. I feel rather authoritative about this subject because, so far as I know, I was the first student of public choice to write a formal analysis showing that corporations, like governments, would not in practice achieve perfection in such areas, although at the same time explaining why one can anticipate that they will come closer to achieving their goals than will government.[1]

---

[1] G. Tullock, 'Welfare Effects of Sales Maximization', *Western Economic Journal*, 1975.

Government and Private Bureaucrats

The government bureaucrat is, in this respect, much like a private sector bureaucrat, in that he will attempt to maximise the well-being of his employer, the state, only if it pays off for him. Similarly, the bureaucrat in General Motors attempts to maximise the return to the stockholders only if that result pays off for him. In neither case is the institutional structure such that perfect reward and punishment systems will drive the bureaucrat into maximising the well-being of his superiors. It happens to be true, however, that the combination of the comparative simplicity of the objective aimed at by stockholders (that they want to make money) and the reasonably accurate methods of measuring the contribution of high-level managers to that end, in the form of the bookkeeping system, make control better in the private sector than it is in the public sector.[2] The United States maintains an embassy in London and McDonald's has stores which sell its hamburgers. It is immensely easier for the management of McDonald's to find out whether their London branches are pursuing profit maximisation than it is for the Department of State to determine whether our embassy in London is performing efficiently.

There is another difference between the slogans 'maximise profit' and 'maximise the public interest'. With the first, there are at least some citizens for whom the goal is of private interest. In the second, there are none. Improving the efficiency of a large corporation by, let us say, 2 per cent may well mean that some individual's wealth goes up by $50 million and a very large number of individuals will achieve increases in wealth of the order of, say, $100 to a million dollars. Maximising the public interest, however, would always be a public good, and an improvement by 2 per cent in the functioning efficiency of some bureau would characteristically increase the well-being of average citizens or, indeed, any citizen by amounts which would be almost invisible. Under the circumstances, one would anticipate that there would be more energy invested in

---

[2] G. Tullock, *The Politics of Bureaucracy*, Washington: Public Affairs Press, 1965. In a way, it is unfortunate that corporations do come fairly close to maximising profit because if they were only to maximise growth instead, everyone except corporate stockholders would be better off.

trying to improve the efficiency of corporations than that of the government. And this is indeed true.

In dealing with the government one does not expect that it will efficiently achieve what we refer to as the 'classical goals' of government. It does not follow from this that it cannot efficiently achieve other goals or, indeed, that with appropriate redesign, it might not achieve some of the classical goals, such as efficient enforcement of the law against assault and battery. Indeed, we can find many cases in which that goal of government has been carried out quite efficiently in the past or, for that matter, is carried out quite efficiently in the present.

The methods of achieving government goals, however, do not appeal to the public interest but to the private interest. We must accept that in government, as in business, people will pursue their own private interests, and they will achieve goals which are reasonably closely related to those of the stockholders or of the citizens only if it is in their private interest to do so. Of course, this does not mean that most people, in addition to pursuing their private interests, have no charitable instincts, tendencies to help others, and to engage in various morally correct activities. Yet, the evidence seems strong that these are not motives upon which we can depend for the motivation of long-continued efficient performance.

Decentralisation and Efficiency

Decentralisation of government and transfer of many activities to a lower level of government can improve efficiency (see Chapter 7). But anyone who looks at the American school system, which is highly decentralised, should realise that it is not in and of itself a magic formula. It seems likely, however, that the combination of two techniques – decentralisation on the purchasing side and competition on the supplying side (see Chapter 2) – would lead to higher efficiency than the present situation, where decentralised units normally provide their own services and the contracting out is mainly done on a centralised, non-competitive basis. It would provide competition on both sides of the market and should lead to improved efficiency.

The only place where this kind of thinking is found in practice is in the 'public utilities' provided in some of our towns and cities by private enterprises. At one time, this was a very common method of provision of public enterprises, but it has steadily shrunk in importance. Apparently the reason that it has shrunk in importance is simply the political power of the employees. They found it easier to get wage increases and other demands by the use of their voting power if the industry (let us say, a street railway system) was transferred to government ownership by the municipality than if it remained in private hands. Nevertheless, what we can see of the remains of this particular market in 'public' services appears to be a good deal more efficient than any other part of our provision of government services.

This conclusion is based on more or less superficial observation. No one has done any careful study of the matter. I should say, however, that the private association where I live, which purchases all sorts of specialised services in a competitive market, does seem to do very well in a price–benefit calculation even though all the people involved in our private 'government' are complete amateurs.

Depriving Bureaucrats of the Vote?
A much more radical conclusion from these discussions of the real motives of bureaucracy is one which, so far as I know, is shared by only a very few students of public choice: that government employees or people who draw the bulk of their income from government by other means should be deprived of the vote. Here the arguments are by no means all on one side, and it seems a very radical proposal to the conventional wisdom. It is a conclusion held almost exclusively by members of the Public Choice Society, and it is not widespread even among that congregation of scholars. It is another example of the opening up of alternatives for investigation and the presentation of new conceivable policy options characteristic of public choice, rather than a policy which all its students favour.

The Size of the Bureau

In my first book on bureaucracy[3], having recently left the Department of State, I offered, as a general rule, that bureaucrats' primary concern is increasing the size of their bureau because that provided a greater opportunity for promotion. I now realise this is an oversimplification because, both in Britain and in the US, there have been cases where the total size of a given bureaucracy shrank without objection from the senior bureaucrats. The cuts, however, generally take place at the bottom of the pyramid, with the senior bureaucrats either gaining, or at least not losing, real income in terms of the attributes they desire from their job.

Many American bureaucracies in the federal government have converted themselves into management and oversight bureaus which devote their time to supervising the work which is done by state and local governments rather than by undertaking any of the work at the federal government level. This change leads to a smaller federal bureaucracy, but also leads to more highly paid positions.

A similar situation has happened in Britain where recent changes benefit the people at the top. I am confident that the effects on themselves are foremost in their minds as the bureaucracies are converted into smaller, more élite organisations. In addition to this stratagem, most bureaucrats have personal ideas about what their agency should be doing which they will relentlessly pursue. Since they are normally dealing with politicians who do not know much about the intricacies of programmes they administer, it is easy to do this. Bureaucrats in the Japanese Ministry of Finance – an exceptionally highly qualified and powerful group of people – pushed the Japanese government into radical changes in the tax laws which also led to major constitutional difficulties in the government process.

The intriguing feature of all this bureaucratic manoeuvring is that the authors of a book about Japanese politics[4], although generally

---

[3] G. Tullock, *The Politics of Bureaucracy*, Washington: Public Affairs Press, 1965.

[4] J. Mark Ramseyer and Frances McCall Rosenbluth, *Japan's Political Marketplace*, Cambridge, Mass: Harvard University Press, 1993.

sympathetic to the Japanese bureaucrats, are unable to explain why they thought this change was desirable. The question is whether they had given serious thought or study to the matter; the answer apparently is they did not. They had a few basic ideas about taxes, absorbed many years ago during the early part of their career in the Ministry.

In a way, the behaviour of members of a bureaucracy resembles people who have a hobby, but with two significant differences. The *first* is that it does not cost the bureaucrats very much since they are predominantly using other people's resources. The *second* is that most of the bureaucrats honestly think that whatever it is they do is *not* for their benefit alone, but for the country or their bureau. They may be right about that, since most bureaucrats are extremely conservative, not in the sense that they are on the right side of the political spectrum, but in the sense that they change only very slowly those ideas they have picked up in the past.

In general, they are largely uninterested in saving money, particularly if the procedure is unpleasant. Some bureaucrats whose sole duty is to reduce the expenditures of other bureaucracies may proceed with considerable enthusiasm, but at least my experience indicates they are totally unwilling to consider reducing the sizes of their own divisions.

Bureaucrats versus Politicians

In the US, and to a lesser extent in Britain, bureaucrats have considerably more power over the politicians who rank above them than the politicians have over them. The bureaucrats themselves, in general, cannot be fired except for some egregious sin. On the other hand, generally speaking, it is not at all difficult for them to make their superiors look very foolish and to sabotage their efforts.

In the US this takes the form of leaking stories to the press which will embarrass the political appointees. It should be pointed out that the press, which wants to maintain its channels of communication with these bureaucrats, will normally put the spin on the story that favours the bureaucracy. Thus, the story which reaches the public may be highly prejudicial to the political appointees.

The Washington Monument Ploy

The Washington monument ploy is an interesting example of bureaucratic action. For the benefit of British readers, I should explain that the story (perhaps a myth) is that on one occasion the US Department of the Interior was told it had to make budget cuts. The response of the bureaucrats was to say the only economy they could think of was to close the Washington Monument so it would no longer provide tours or access to tourists. During the recent partial shutdown of the US government, the operations of the Smithsonian's Air and Space Museum were restricted to the lobby, the gift shop and the restroom. Before the collapse of the Communist régimes, the US military forces held a defensive position against a potential attack by the Russians through Germany. The front line of the US position was covered by a cavalry regiment with light, fast-moving vehicles and very good radio interception equipment. They were there, of course, to give first warning of an attack. The US Army in Europe also maintained a number of military bands to play for official functions and parades. When pressed to suggest ways of cutting the budget, the military always listed the light cavalry regiment as the first unit to be cut without mentioning any of its military bands. They, of course, felt confident that their political superiors would not cut the cavalry.

Politicians are aware of this kind of bureaucractic deception, but they also know that they can be seriously embarrassed by the bureaucrats leaking unpleasant information or, even, disinformation. Because they also know they cannot fire the bureaucrats, it is understandable that they are unable to maintain discipline over their 'inferiors'. Granted the history of political spoilsmanship, it is not obvious that the present system is worse, but it obviously has its defects.

Bureaucrats and Pressure Groups

Bureaucrats frequently form mutually beneficial alliances with pressure groups. The obvious case is the Department of Agriculture and the farm lobby, but there are many more. Furthermore, the relevant government committees in Congress are also part of this conspiracy. It is called the 'iron triangle' in the standard literature. In agriculture, this was particularly clear because both the Senate and the House of Representatives had agricultural committees which dealt both with the subsidy scheme and the appropriations of the Department of Agriculture. The Department spent large sums of money improving crop yields followed by large sums of money to take the newly-produced goods off the market to prevent prices from falling.

The same phenomenon can be found in many other programmes. The bureaucracies almost uniformly regard themselves as, among other things, special pleaders in Washington for the particular group of people they benefit. J. Edgar Hoover was frequently criticised for his politics, but I am sure from his own perspective (he came from a bureaucratic family) that taking a small, relatively inoffensive group of people, mostly accountants, and converting it into the powerful structure we see today was a major achievement. It was bureaucratic imperialism at its most brilliant.

Summary

To sum up, most public choice scholars do not think that government is systematically engaged in maximising the public interest, but assume that the government officials are attempting to maximise their own private interests. In this, of course, they are like managers of United States Steel. Most people probably feel that, both in the private market and in the government sector, there are institutions which tend to lead individuals, maximising their own interests, at least to some extent to provide goods for other people as a by-product. In neither case is the institutional structure so designed that perfection is obtained. My criticism of bureaucrats is, I should emphasise, not that they are bad people. Indeed, in most well-established societies, Washington for example, bureaucrats represent a collection of, generally, pleasant people. Indeed, in Washington, they lead a pleasant social life. They are the types of people you would much enjoy knowing. It is the institutional situation in which they find themselves that frees them from the constraint of efficiently carrying out the tasks to which they have been assigned. This quite obviously makes the bureaus less than optimally efficient. Further, they can make considerable gains in terms of their personal preferences by underplaying the preferences of their theoretical 'masters'.

Large governments, or for that matter large private corporations, must have bureaucracies. Of necessity, the objectives of the bureaucracy are never exactly those of their superiors. There is no doubt they can be a big help to good government. They can also be a large impediment.

6

TAX AVOISION

IN THE LITERATURE ABOUT TAXES, there are frequent references to the terms 'tax avoidance' and 'tax evasion'. Arthur Seldon dealt with this problem by combining the two words to create the new word 'avoision' which is in the title of this chapter. This chapter sets out to develop the implications of this new term which captures both tax avoidance and tax evasion as methods of reducing your total tax payment in one word. Roughly speaking, tax avoidance is taking measures to reduce your tax liability which are perfectly legal. Tax evasion, on the other hand, refers to the use of illegal means to lower your tax liability. Both have implications for resource allocations for society and the behavioural choice of tax-payers. We will consider them one at a time, beginning with tax avoidance.

The Home Mortgage Deduction

Consider the following simple example of tax avoidance under United States tax law. Homeowners who have mortgages may deduct the interest on the mortgage from their taxable income. The mortgage deduction, the largest 'loophole' in the US Tax Code, works for people in all tax brackets. Although it now has immense political support it originally got into the income tax laws more or less by accident. The reason that this example of tax avoidance leads to inefficiency can perhaps best be shown by considering my own situation. I am a bachelor and, for the past 15 years, I have owned either the house or apartment in which I lived subject to as large a mortgage as I can talk bankers into lending me. If I rented a house or apartment, I would not be able to avoid taxes because I would not be paying interest; and rent on a house is not deductible.

I save a great deal of money which would have been paid in taxes through this provision, even though a person who moves as often as

I might be equally satisfied with rental housing.[1] The same is true for many people. Americans do move a good deal, but even those who do not move frequently tended to rent their quarters until the Second World War when income tax rates rose enough to make the saving significant from the interest deduction on a mortgage.

There is no doubt that moving from one place to another if you have to sell one property and buy another is much less convenient than just dropping one lease and entering another. It is also expensive for the middle class. As a consequence the avoidance of taxes, which I reiterate is purely legal in this example, does inflict a cost on society.

The Cost of Loopholes

The reader may feel that the home mortgage interest deduction is not a gigantic inefficiency inflicted upon the economy. It is probable that the total reduction in taxes from this loophole is sizeable. Some would further argue that, after all, 'if you give the money to the government it will only waste it'. Any major cost imposed by this loophole comes from people modifying their behaviour (buying houses rather than renting them) to avoid taxes. When we turn to the illegal evasion methods later in this chapter, you will find that the same question can be asked, but that it results in a different answer.

Let us examine the possible costs of these loopholes. The first obvious effect is that if the taxes are left at the same level as they would be without the loophole, the government would have less to spend. In spite of my earlier remark about government waste, this reduction in tax revenues may lead to underfinancing of genuinely valuable programmes. Of course, it may also lead to underfinancing of programmes which we would be better off without.

There is another possibility which is a more likely outcome. The government response to an income tax loophole which removes $50 million annually from tax revenues may simply be to raise the basic tax rate such that the tax system with this loophole produces the same

---

[1] A newspaper article noted 'a fast growing breed of professionals nationwide who, fed up with the high cost and low return of home ownership, are choosing to rent apartments'. (K. Blumenthal,'Luxury-Apartment rentals are booming', *The Wall Street Journal*, 22 September 1995, p. B1.)

tax revenues as it had before. The government would provide the same set of services as before: the difference is mainly that the cost of the loophole is distributed in a different way among taxpayers through the tax system. In cases where the government is both setting the base tax rate and producing this loophole, there is no reason to believe that accepting the loophole or raising other taxes to compensate for its loss would be more efficient than the other. In practice, however, what probably happens is a compromise in which both useful and valueless programmes are cut back.

The cost of such loopholes is difficult to calculate. It should be said that most people find them annoying in terms of their effects and in the difficulty of understanding them. Until a few years ago the United States Tax Code contained 17 pages devoted to the raising of race-horses.[2] This seemed to most people simply a detailed discussion of a particular industry. However, when this section was repealed the effect was significant. The value of breeding stock fell, by more than 50 per cent in some cases. In other words, these 17 pages had the effect of reducing the cost of raising race-horses very sharply, attracting new investors, and in increasing the price of breeding stock as capital.

We can find many other cases of this sort in which the economy is distorted by the existence of tax advantages. One element of the tax code which affects wealthy people more than any other is simply taking long vacations. On a vacation I would not be earning money, but I would presumably be getting as much pleasure out of my vacation as from the income I would otherwise earn. If this were not true, I would not take the vacation. Because leisure is not taxed, I avoid taxes by taking vacations. Given a choice between an income of $500,000 per year with the traditional two-week vacation or an income of $450,000 with seven weeks of vacation, I might choose the $500,000. However, if there is a 50 per cent tax rate on earnings above $100,000, the net income after taxes is $300,000 versus $275,000.[3] As a consequence, I might choose the job with the longer

---

[2] The United States Tax Code and the regulations issued to interpret it are sufficiently lengthy that I doubt any one has read all the way through them.

[3] These numbers are arbitrary, but not too different from the United States Tax Code.

vacation. It seems likely that high income earners, whether executives or television stars, allocate their time between work and leisure so this causes a social loss.

The cost to society of the behavioural incentives of the tax code is presumably the product that I would have made had I worked full time. That people will take more vacations under a higher tax system than with lower taxes is clear. Another outcome may be that people simply do not work as hard. The net effect is to reduce society's income.

Special Services for the Tax Industry

Let us consider another outcome of tax avoision in that there are a very large number of industries (other than producing race-horses) which exist solely for the purpose of providing tax exemptions. Medical doctors and other professionals frequently attend conferences in quite pleasant and expensive resorts, sometimes even on luxury ocean liners. As long as the conference programme has the appearance that something is learned or otherwise some economic gain is made, the individual's cost of attending such conferences is deductible from income taxes. This means that conferences cost the person attending a good deal less than they otherwise would and that people will take more of these semi-vacations than they would if their income was reduced by the full cost.

Corporate Structure as a Response to the Tax System

There are many other examples of the effects of the tax code on individual behaviour. The author is involved with a family-owned company in Iowa. Though the company is small, it has a most elaborate corporate structure, designed for us by a tax accountant, which does indeed reduce our taxes. However, it is clearly less efficient than a simple corporate structure in that resources are invested in meeting the tax provisions that might produce higher returns in another investment.

Another problem related to corporate income taxes is that if the corporation is financed with common stock, the income of the owners is taxed at corporate rates. But, if the corporation is financed by selling bonds, the interest on the bonds is deductible as a business expense. This encourages most corporations to finance a larger proportion of their investments by selling bonds than is desirable from the standpoint of economic efficiency.

No doubt, one could continue listing these distortions resulting from the tax code. In most cases the reduction in economic efficiency and the taxes avoided by the individual or corporation are comparatively small. Nevertheless, it is clear that the economy is less efficient than it would be in the absence of these incentives for tax avoision. The efficiency loss implies that the government would either collect less tax revenues, which by itself would pressure bureaucrats to be more efficient, or that a government would use a tax system such as a value-added tax without exemptions which permit tax avoision.[4]

Tax Evasion

The second element in this chapter on tax avoision is the simple, straightforward evasion of taxes. Let us begin with some rather obvious cases of evasion. Tax evasion is often thought of as simply under-reporting of income to tax authorities. The income may be legally obtained or from illegal activities such as the sale of drugs, certain types of gambling, sexual services, or stolen goods.[5] The term 'black' or 'underground' economy describes the activities used by people to evade taxes. People who engage in these illegal activities obviously do not pay income tax in most cases. It should be said that in the United States some members of the mafia who are very well off pay income tax for the purpose of explaining to the Internal Revenue Service why they have an obviously high standard of living. Normally they claim their income is based on legal forms of gambling such as horse racing.

---

[4] There are not any such systems in the real world.

[5] Strictly speaking, evasion would also include activities to avoid state excise taxes on liquor and cigarettes by buying large quantities in states with low excise taxes.

The cost of the underground economy
That this kind of tax avoision on the whole is undesirable is obvious, but the undesirability of concealing your income from criminal activities is less important than the criminal activities themselves. Nevertheless, it is likely that in the United States there is a significant amount of income derived from such illegal activities that is not taxed. The underground economy is believed to be as large as 5–10 per cent of the United States Gross Disposable Product ($300 to $600 billion for 1993).[6] Needless to say, I object not to the tax avoision aspects of such activities, but to the activities themselves. If they were taxed, the profits from such illegal activities would be lower and hence fewer people would enter the 'industry.'

Although taxing this form of tax avoision would add to the national budget, it is not a gigantic amount. On the other hand, in some other form it is likely to be much larger. A former minister of finance in Italy once suggested to me that Italy probably had as high a living standard as West Germany, even though their statistics did not show it. He explained that the difference was the black economy, which at that time would have to have been almost 50 per cent of total economic activity in order to balance the national income numbers. This is not impossible as any one who has visited Italy can attest, although I think perhaps he was being a bit too optimistic about Italian prosperity

The existence of tax avoision from the black economy raises a number of philosophical problems. Suppose I need some minor repairs around my house. Although I am unskilled in making repairs, there are some things I could do, although it would take me more time and the results would probably not be as good as if I had hired some one. Nevertheless, under the United States Tax Code, if I perform the repairs myself there is no tax to be paid, but this could to some extent reduce my income from my regular employment since such repair work is not rest and recreation for most of us. A third possibility is that I hire a repairman, but he

---

[6] For a survey of the size of 'black' economies see Friedrich Schneider and Dominik H. Enste, 'Shadow Economies: Sizes, Causes and Consequences', *Journal of Economic Literature*, Vol. 38 (1) pp. 77–114, March 2000.

conceals the matter from the government in order to evade paying taxes.

From the standpoint of our own interest, the third example is clearly the best. The repairman is undoubtedly better at doing the job than I am, and he will no doubt perform the work for less money since he has chosen to conceal the income from taxes. Is there any real reason why we should object to this form of tax avoision? The answer to this question may depend on whether you believe the government needs the money. If you feel it does not, you might argue that it would be better to change the tax structure so that it gets less, and have this kind of avoision eliminated.

Nevertheless, this kind of avoision is a large-scale activity in much of the world. I understand that even Sweden has a great deal of it. Tax avoision is so common that it is not clear in my mind whether I encourage it or not. For example, I have a cleaning lady who comes once a week, and periodically I hire some one for minor repairs. The amounts are small enough so that under the United States Tax Code, I am not required to report the payments, although if the law were carried out, the recipients would report them as income.[7] I have never inquired whether they do so.

A Social Cost of Avoision

It is very difficult to determine which of these three is socially desirable because one would have to know what the government would do if the law were strictly carried out and the additional taxes were collected and made available for expenditures. For example, would the government use the additional revenue for the purpose of reducing some other tax? I doubt it, but it is possible. Or would the government use the money to do something which produces more benefits than the cost? Once again, I doubt it, but cannot be certain.

---

[7] Failure to pay social security taxes on the wages of domestic employees became an issue in the appointment of several political officials. The adverse publicity was sufficient to complicate and in some cases derail the appointment.

Hernando De Soto's *The Other Path* is an important book which is available in both English and Spanish.[8] He estimates that the black market, or as he calls it the informal market, accounts for roughly half of economic activity in Peru. He views it in a positive light and as helping the poor to raise the income of the poor. In general, De Soto argues that in many of the less advanced parts of the world similar situations exist with the unreported economy. On my last visit to Rio de Janeiro I stayed in the same hotel that I stayed in five years' earlier. The hill overlooking the hotel provides a good example of this phenomenon. People had built houses which were actually on government land rather than on private land. Following the South American tradition, they had set up a government of their own, and since my last visit, made such 'public' improvements as sidewalks and a flight of stairs. Due to the topography of the location, it was not possible for roads to be put in. No doubt, this is an improvement in the economy of Brazil. I have no doubt that it neither appears in their official economic statistics nor do the inhabitants pay taxes.

Concluding Comments

The end-product of all of this is, unfortunately, that there are no clear conclusions. In general, people frown on the 'tax cheater', but it is not clear that such tax avoision actually harms anyone. Its mere existence increases the total product of the nation, although not necessarily the formal GDP. Furthermore, if the people concerned were engaged in 'non-black' production, they would make a larger social contribution. Finally, their mere existence puts a certain amount of restraint on the government. Whether the restraint is good or bad depends in essence on what the government does.

---

[8] *The Other Path: The Invisible Revolution in the Third World.* Hernando de Soto, I. B. Tauris, 1989. I recommend this important book to everyone interested in the topic.

7

FEDERALISM

'FEDERALISM' IS USUALLY ASSOCIATED WITH EITHER
THE AMERICAN OR THE SWISS GOVERNMENT, but there are
many other examples in the world. Basically, it means a division of
governments between centralised functions and those programmes
more efficiently provided locally. Economic theory demonstrates
that some types of public goods (police, fire protection, sewers,
schools) should have many providers while for public goods with
different characteristics (such as national defence), one government
provider is justified. The term federalism has come to mean the
optimal layering or decentralisation of existing government services
based on an examination of possible economies of scale. The
'appropriate' governmental unit is designated on the basis of least
cost or efficiency. Scale economies are an element of the supply side
and provide no insight into the services people might actually want.
A more productive inquiry is to ask: 'What do we want out of
government?'

Voters' Preferences

This approach recognises that voters have diverse preferences, and
that what we really want is a government that is responsive to the
people's desires as well as one that provides services efficiently.
Economic efficiency and the diverse preferences of voters in a large
country such as the United States may often appear contradictory
terms. This chapter will explore the tensions between these aims.
Some voters, for example, want public provision of jogging paths
and outdoor recreational areas; others may want the Internet and
well-stocked community libraries. Still others may seek pristine
environmental amenities and a risk-minimising society, while others
may seek to make choices based on their benefits and costs.
An important implication is that the higher the degree of diverse

preferences among voters the less likely is it that any one government will please everyone.

Consider the situation of the author of this chapter. I am a citizen with powers to vote in the United States, in the State of Arizona, and in Pima County. Further, a number of small school systems in Pima County have organised an entity called the Tucson Unified School District which is controlled by an elected board for which I can vote. Each of these 'governments' controls some aspect of the society in which I live. In the United States, a great deal more of the services generally provided by governments may be provided through private market activities. In addition to schooling, such services may include medical care, personal security, parcel delivery, fire protection, refuse removal, water, and privately financed highways.

Degrees of Decentralisation

All national governments, of course, exhibit some degree of decentralisation. It was not possible for the Emperor of China to make personal decisions on such matters as whether a particular small bridge should be repaired. Decentralisation may take the form, as it did in most of the world, of simply designating civil servants with authority over various government functions. The Union of South Africa, before its recent constitutional change, was, for example, nominally a union of four states, but the governments of these states comprised simply civil servants dispatched from the central government. Interestingly enough China, which remains a despotism, used civil servants to manage services in local counties, while small villages and the neighbourhoods within the large cities were self-governing.

In recent years two opposite trends in federalism have emerged. A number of centralised nations, such as France, have shifted powers from central to local governments. While this has been going on in a formal way, there has been a tendency for revenue and hence political power to shift upward. Let us consider the United States. In 1900 the total apparatus of government was much smaller than it is now, but the federal government made up only about one-third of the total. Currently, with much larger government at all levels, the federal government makes up about two-thirds of local and federal expenditures.

Further, the federal government exercises much additional control over the local governments by a number of orders and laws. The past several years have witnessed the emergence of the 'unfunded mandate' as a major political issue in which the federal government merely requires the states to provide specific services, but provides no funding. In the opinion of this author, the shift of power to the local areas in France was a step in the right direction and the increasing power of the central government through expansive policies and unfunded mandates in the United States, a step in the wrong direction.[1]

I frequently learn in talking with people who are not accustomed to federalism that they think decentralised governments cannot be as efficient as centralised governments. Apparently, they mistake efficiency for what I might call 'pomp and circumstance'. It is true that California is as large as many nations throughout the world. Yet, at the other extreme, Switzerland, which is no bigger than many of the states in the United States, is divided into cantons, some very small. As far as I know, the Swiss government is not criticised for being inefficient or disorderly. Indeed, the general vision of Switzerland is of a very well-administered (small) country.

Basics of Federalism

The basic argument for federalism is simply that there are many government activities for which there is no particular need to have a national policy. Consider, for example, the road system. In the United States, the interstate system and earlier the national highway system, were originally designed primarily by the national government in co-operation with the states. At the moment they are maintained and improved from time to time, primarily by the state governments using funds from the federal government under some degree of federal co-ordination of the overall system.

---

[1] For further elaboration on this point, see G. Tullock, *The New Federalist*, Vancouver, BC: Fraser Institute, 1995 (also available in Serbo-Croat, Russian and Korean).

Purely Local Decisions
Aside from the Interstate Highway System, we find ourselves confronted at one extreme by a large number of state highways which are primarily built and maintained by the state and at the other by a lot of local streets built and maintained[2] by the county or the city. When we talk about the federal government co-ordinating the states it should be kept in mind that the US federal government is dominated by a group of people who are elected from local constituencies. Thus, the decision by the federal government to do something in the state of Arizona is probably influenced heavily by the Senators and Members of the House of Representatives from Arizona. Nevertheless, the central government has a different perspective from that of the local governments. Drivers in Tucson have been severely inconvenienced by a project to improve Tanque Verde Road. They do not seem unduly disturbed by the inconvenient routes which the project necessitates. No doubt they all expect to be better off after the road is finished.

There is no reason why anyone except the people who live in Tucson should be interested in the inconvenience or improvements in Tanque Verde Road. Undoubtedly, leaving this purely local decision to those most closely involved is a more efficient way of dealing with the local transport system than to have a group of federal bureaucrats bargain with the Senators and Congressmen who make the decisions about such projects as Tanque Verde Road.

The Importance of the Popular Vote
In the United States, and even more in Switzerland, there are direct popular votes on many purely local issues. New school buildings and major road developments are frequently submitted to the voters of the city or county. It seems obvious that this way of dealing with local issues and projects works better than first delegating power by

---

[2] New developments normally have their streets built by the developer with only minimal supervision from the city or county. The streets will then either be deeded to the city or county government or to a private community association of homeowners.

election to the central government and then the federal government redelegating this power to its civil servants in Tucson.

There is a more theoretical argument in favour of federalism. The individual voter in the United States is one in about 70 million when it comes to voting for the President. That his individual influence is not large is obvious. As we move to smaller and smaller government, however, the likelihood that a given voter, or a given small group of voters with some particular unifying interest, will be important to an individual politician steadily increases. Four or five hundred voters concerned about some issue in their neighbourhood will receive the attention of the county board of supervisors. But they will have very little influence with either the state or the national government. It is likely that a diversified set of purely local decisions with each local governmental unit having the attention of locally responsible and politically accountable elected officials is more efficient than a centralised decision process.[3]

Voting with the Feet

Two of the advantages of decentralisation that federalism permits are not directly concerned with voting. The first of these is 'voting with the feet'. Because it is possible for a resident to choose where he lives or where he will locate his business, this choice in markets puts the various local governments in competition with each other. Since their tax revenue depends upon how many people live or work within their boundaries, it brings market considerations to bear on government and provides individuals with two important ways to influence the local government decisions. First, they can choose where they will live, and then they have a vote in the affairs of the government of that area. Picking a place which is agreeable to them

---

[3] We see this trend in Britain as the functions of county councils are taken over by cities. 'The Local Government Commission for England, after its third review of local authorities since 1992, announced that seven other large towns would become unitary – meaning they will take over control of education and social services from their county councils.' (J. Authers, 'Regeneration pushes local council shake-up', *Financial Times*, 27 September 1995, p. 13.)

and then working to make it more agreeable gives them more control than if they had only one way of dealing with the matter.

Readers will no doubt remember that during President John F. Kennedy's administration East Germany was being 'depopulated' by its citizens voting with their feet. The communist response was the Berlin Wall which permitted them to have a governmental system which was vastly inferior to that in the West, and at the same time made it impossible for their subjects simply to depart. The collapse of the wall was regarded by everyone, with the possible exception of some East German government officials, as a major improvement.

Obviously, the situation in a non-federal state is not the same, although local governments are subject to pressure to be as efficient as their neighbours. Local city government is subject to pressure to be attractive to both its residents and potential new entrants. In reading *The Economist* I frequently see advertisements by local governments to attract businesses to locate within their bounds, although there does not seem to be much effort to attract individual citizens. In the United States the same search for businesses occurs but in our case there is a positive effort to attract individual citizens as well.

Responding to Demand

A second feature of federalism is that it permits the development of specialised government structures and services to attract specific types of people. The suburbs which surround large American cities often compete by providing higher expenditure on public services in order to attract people and businesses. For example, New Trier, a Chicago suburb, has for generations maintained a superb school system. The tax cost to the residents is very high; the residents apparently like what they get. Large numbers of parents move into New Trier when their oldest child reaches the age to enter school, and then move out as soon as the youngest child has graduated.

The Role of Competition

Competition is a basic feature of federalism. We find somewhat similar competition among the states. Mississippi recently had a campaign to improve its schools with the intention to attract industry.

79

Needless to say, other states regarded this type of competition as unfortunate, but the standpoint of the citizenry is that it is a good idea for cities and states to compete in providing superior service at low tax cost. Such competition to attract specific groups may distress 'socialists' and others who do not favour market processes. Civil servants also dislike being under a kind of competition. But for those interested in the well-being of the citizen, the efficiency of government in putting officials under this kind of pressure works well.

Making Comparisons Easy
There is another way to put the governmental officials under competitive pressures. Comparisons among governments are relatively easy. Most voters are not adept at examining elaborate theoretical and empirical evidence on the efficiency of governments. They do know what taxes they are paying and they also know what services the government is providing to them, but without a basis for comparison they do not know whether this is efficient or not.

In a federal system, they can make direct comparisons with the neighbouring city or school district. The Tucson Unified School District, mentioned above, is not in complete control of all schools in its area. Because several small suburbs maintain their own schools, they put the Tucson Unified School District under continuous pressure to respond to those parents who may vote with their feet. A very large number of the voters in the elections of the Tucson Unified School District live close to the borders of these small communities so that the education that their children are getting can be compared with the education that is provided in those communities.

As mentioned above, this competition goes across states. Every year various standardised tests are given to students all over the United States, and newspapers carry stories about the average scores both in cities and in states. This again provides a low-cost basis for comparing educational systems. Honesty compels me to admit that almost 90 per cent of all American school systems report that the students are 'above average'. Still, how much above average varies among the school systems, and the ordinary newspaper reader can readily become aware of this difference and put pressure on his state and local government to improve.

If little Johnny is not doing as well as his friend Edward, who lives across the boundary in another school district, the parents are apt to know it and complain. All of this gives an incentive to the civil servants to improve the services. After all, they can be fired locally and it does not require an elaborate appeal process to Washington to get rid of them.

Contracting Out

Many people will feel that relatively small government cannot obtain the economies of scale which would be available to larger government. This is true if the small community tries to do everything itself; but if it is also willing to contract out private services – and most communities are – this is not true. The area around Los Angeles has been particularly effective in contracting with the private sector for various services. For example, the city government of Lakewood, a Los Angeles suburb, consisted of the city council, one engineer and one secretary with all other functions contracted out. Indeed, the duties of the engineer and secretary consisted primarily of organising contracts. Lakewood contracted with the Los Angeles Sheriff's office for policing, taxes were collected by the City of Los Angeles, and many other services were contracted out either to other governments or to the private sector. It is of some interest that the Sheriff's Office of Los Angeles charges the city of Lakewood less per 'patrol car unit' than it does its own citizens. It faced competition in Lakewood and not in the county of Los Angeles where it had direct control. Hence, there was a lower price in Lakewood.

Lakewood is an extreme case, but there are many more similar examples. I live in a small community of about 500 houses which receives fire protection from the Rural/Metro Fire Company. This private service happens to be a technological leader in fire protection having invented a great deal of new technology. For example, our fire hydrants are twice as far apart as would be the case for conventional equipment. Because their pumpers are able to operate at much wider intervals, fewer hydrants are needed and they charge roughly half of the tax cost imposed on similar houses within the city of Tucson where fire protection is provided by the local government. In this case the economies of scale are in favour of my small community, not the City of Tucson. Rural/Metro provides a total amount of fire protection which is probably three or four times as high as that provided by the City and it does this scattered all over the state of Arizona.

Most government activities can be handled by private contracting. Waste disposal is probably the largest single example, but all sorts of other services are contracted out, including the provision of prisons and much of pollution control. In general, the reason more contracting out does not occur is that the entrenched civil servants do not like the idea of losing their jobs. The companies that offer fire protection, and so on, do not like the idea of losing their contracts either, but as a rule of thumb the local governments are unwilling to offer long-term contracts. It is almost a custom, for example, that fire protection contracts between companies and small cities are drawn up for five years with complete reconsideration at the end of the period. My view is that this period is long enough to permit the companies to make the capital investments they need and short enough so they do not become over-confident.

Conclusions

I began this chapter by saying that under modern circumstances, it would appear that centralised control is being replaced by local control. Yet, for many services, the central government is growing more rapidly than local governments rather than shedding its employees. Given the decentralising advantages of federalism, I find this somewhat mysterious, but I am also quite convinced that it is an undesirable development. In general, a central government should provide only those few activities where external benefits are very large. Otherwise, we are better off with small government units. A mix of different sized governmental units designed for different functions is optimal.

The reason for this conflict between the efficiency considerations and the actual movement in many places is not obvious. It is particularly difficult because federalism as a decentralisation of government in theory has had quite a good press in recent years. If DeGaulle was in favour of it, as he was, how could anyone be found who is against it?

There seem to be several reasons, although I am not clear exactly why this development has occurred. The *first* is the myth that central government is more efficient. *Second*, this myth has appeared despite the superior efficiency of local government in many activities, largely because local officials hired economically by local governments are not very polished. A *third* reason is the continuous pressure by the bureaucracy for central control. The central bureaucrats obviously want to increase their power and local bureaucrats frequently would like to be part of the federal government and hence push in the same direction.

But these tendencies, I think, are minor. The major reason for increasing federalism in the USA is an intellectual mistake made by most voters. They almost seem to believe that central government expenditures come from the tooth fairy. They press for various local projects 'paid for' by the central government. Those particular projects are desirable from their standpoint because most of the cost is paid for by taxes collected from other local governments else-where. They apparently feel that if they do not push for their projects, they will still have to pay taxes to support projects in other parts of the country. The whole collection is to their disadvantage, but what they see – a local project and the low local cost – is to their advantage. The tendency to federalism for this reason is an indirect effect of log-rolling.

But all of this is not the whole explanation. I suspect that we have here a simple example of the way public opinion may sometimes be misled by people simply repeating some popular conventional wisdom. Not very long ago most people, including most intellectuals, thought that socialism was more efficient than democracy. This was an example of people simply picking up the current fashion, which in turn was picked up as current wisdom. At the moment, the current wisdom with respect to socialism is the opposite, and we can hope for a similar favourable change in attitudes towards federalism.

PART II

AMERICAN APPLICATIONS

Gordon L. Brady

1

PROTECTION IN

INTERNATIONAL TRADE

Introduction

PART II ON AMERICAN APPLICATIONS BEGINS WITH PROTECTIONISM because it illustrates some very powerful public choice insights, showing how institutions affect the ability of producers to secure tariffs or other special privileges. The fundamental condition is that small consumers are many and unorganised while producers are few and better organised. The degree to which conditions and institutions give rise to special privileges will differ from country to country and from industry to industry, but the fundamentals do not change. In every country it is in the self-interest of consumers to buy whatever they want from suppliers who sell it cheapest. Many domestic producers, however, are harmed by competition from foreign suppliers under free trade and would benefit from protective measures to restrict imports.

From the time of David Ricardo in the early 19th century most competent economists have judged that protective tariffs are unwise, except under exceptional circumstances. The original 16th- and 17th-century mercantilist arguments against free trade were called into question by Adam Smith and refuted by Ricardo, but they have continued to influence policy in Europe and the United States up to the present day. They are not yet dead. The paradox of protection is epitomised in the following question: Why do people who are injured by protection apparently think that it is, on the whole, somehow beneficial to them? Such apparently irrational thoughts often serve as the intellectual basis for national political policies of protection. The expectation of gain in excess of cost leads special-interest groups to persuade governments into implementing national protectionist policies regardless of the harmful effects on society as a whole. These interest groups seek to build public support by self-serving arguments that protectionist policies promote the national interest by 'levelling the playing field', protecting specific strategic industries from foreign competition, strengthening 'infant industries' to create economic growth, preserving jobs, and other specious arguments.

Given the ingenuity of politicians in government, it is not surprising that protection is still created by tariffs, quotas, and other non-tariff restrictions on international trade. In addition to direct payments, tax write-offs, or favourable regulatory advantages for domestic producers, protection may include anti-dumping regulations and rules that promote health, safety, and 'environmental' objectives. Protection may be obtained by the creation of regulatory barriers in the form of 'red tape', regulations and technical specifications or standards. Costly and time-consuming paperwork is an obvious example of an impediment to international trade.

Logrolling, Rent Seeking, and Rational Ignorance

Public choice provides two (related) explanations for the demand for and supply of protection: logrolling, which entails 'trading of votes' among politicians, and rent seeking, which involves lobbying and other efforts to obtain governmentally bestowed international trade restrictions. As discussed in Part I, Chapter 3, logrolling is a form of exchange in which votes are traded on the basis of promises made at various points in time. The mechanism for the exchange is the legislature: Congress, Parliament, Knesset and others.

Representatives in a legislature are constantly making deals with one another though they are rarely explicit in specific legislation. Arrangements may stretch over several years and, since they are promises, the rational legislator may breach them. Trades often take the form that the protection for a completely unrelated industry in, say, Virginia may be traded for a dam in Wyoming or an irrigation project in Arizona. In turn, dams in one district are traded off against the extension of an existing programme or a new programme offering special interest pay-offs.

Most economists view logrolling in the abstract as enhancing welfare. That vote-trading enables representatives to register the intensity of their preferences between various legislative proposals is well recognised among economists. With regard to international trade, however, logrolling may have the harmful effect of allowing import protection for one regional industry (South Carolina textile quotas, for example) to be traded for protection of another regional industry (perhaps quotas for Louisiana sugar producers). Theories based on collective action generally conclude that small well-organised groups have an advantage, even when cost-benefit calculations do not support protection.

Protection is a form of rent seeking which involves the pursuit of special privilege from government. An example will allow us to see the difficulty of dealing with protection and illustrates the misguided basis of much of the domestic response to protection. In October 1997, the US sought to impose fines on Japanese shippers in retaliation for Japanese restrictions on US access to Japanese port facilities. The 'protection' resulted from Japanese port practices which preserved inefficient bureaucracy and labour methods, and served the interests of trade unions and organised crime.

The Japanese shippers receive the benefits of the restrictions but also incur higher costs for shipping. Nor are the results those intended by the US. In this case, the fines imposed on Japanese shipping lines which use US facilities punish the victims of the Japanese port practices rather than the perpetrators. Countering protection in this case is not simple because the US does not have legal access to the Japanese interest groups causing the protection.

US threats to close US ports to Japanese vessels would almost certainly violate World Trade Organisation (WTO) rules which preclude such antagonistic sanctions. The basis for the US closure is the Jones Act, a protectionist law passed in 1920 that guarantees US-built and -owned vessels a monopoly of the country's shipping industry. The US ignored the opportunity to discuss this matter during the WTO negotiations on maritime services in 1995 because of opposition from beneficiaries of the Jones Act. Efforts to protect the beneficiaries of the Jones Act also kept the US from ratifying a draft Organisation for Economic Co-operation and Development (OECD) treaty to curb shipbuilding subsidies.

Product Standards and Free Trade

The specification of product performance standards, such as those governing automobile emissions, industrial effluents, energy consumption, or size and weight limitations on agricultural products, can act as more subtle, but equally damaging, impediments to free trade. Product design standards that differ in ways that make selling products difficult may be a less obvious, but nonetheless an unintended and significant, form of protection. Britain requires cars to drive on the left side of the highway so steering wheels are on the right, while in continental Europe the opposite prevails. As a consequence, residents of Britain are less likely to shop for an automobile in continental Europe. Differences in environmental and emissions standards may also dictate design features that serve to limit the markets, for instance, for motor cars. Other design features governing the manufacture of such products as television sets, video tape players, and electrical equipment differ among nations and thus serve as impediments to international trade.

The health of animals and plants has also earned the attention of the advocates of protection. Imports of agricultural products can be barred outright or made more costly by mandatory testing on the grounds that they may have, or may be imagined to have, diseases (as with British beef) or parasites which can spread to domestic plants and animals. Regulations which restrict agricultural imports have also been used by various special-interest groups to promote other goals, such as animal rights or the eradication of the anthrax bacterium which causes 'mad cow' disease.

In recent years, protectionists have found new arguments which are based on the danger to the environment. One line of argument stresses the protection of the global environment through international trade restrictions designed to prevent other countries from obtaining an advantage by relatively less stringent regulations on environmental quality management.

Regulations designed to protect public health, food safety, and the environment may be justified. The kind of quarantine the US used to impose on human beings who came from plague spots might reasonably be imposed on imports of fruit and vegetables. Furthermore, it may be difficult to tell whether a foreign insect, which could be a major pest in the US, has deposited eggs under the surface of, say, an imported apple. If preventing an infestation is the objective, requiring that each individual apple be carefully inspected would be a better policy than a tariff that affects only the domestic price.

Interest Groups, Logrolling, and Protection

The public choice economist encounters little difficulty in explaining why the automobile or agricultural industry wants a tariff or quota on imported automobiles or agricultural products. Because the beneficiaries of protection are concentrated and small in number, and the cost of the tariff or quota is widely diffused among consumers of the product and the tax-payers (who pay for the administration), one might expect such efforts would be politically successful.

Various interest groups continue to foster policies which have the effect of raising the price that domestic producers may charge despite the advantages which free trade offers consumers. Protectionist policies succeed because individual consumers suffer insufficient harm to overcome the transactions costs of becoming organised in opposition to the policy. Moreover, once protectionist measures are established by government, they assume a life of their own. They can be expected to persist as special interests mobilise to prevent the erosion of special privilege. The rent-seeking element of protection explains the activities of special interests seeking benefits at the expense of the general public.

As previously explained, logrolling enables representatives to register the intensity of their preferences among issues. A representative who feels strongly about animal rights can 'trade' his vote on issues about which he does not feel so intensely. While logrolling would appear beneficial to the legislators, its general efficiency depends on the political setting. Because most legislatures are based on geographic representation, a representative's re-election depends on how well he represents the interests of his district. Because the US Congress is a geographically based institution, the incentive of the legislator is to represent the interest of the district from which he is elected at the expense of broader national interests.

Most members of a community share an interest in well-being and will be sensitive to the local impact of national policies. There are often political settings with blocs of voters whose income depends upon such geographically concentrated industries as steel, automobiles, defence, or agriculture. When economic activity is concentrated in a small geographic area, Congressmen can obtain political support by serving the economic interest of their district. Tariffs, tax concessions for specific industries, public works projects such as highway-building, or contracts with local industries for defence-related items (military bases or the manufacture of equipment) are examples of issues decided on the basis of their economic impact on specific regions and industries.

In some circumstances, the rational politician may even trade his/her support on national issues (such as the environment, defence, and trade protection) for support from other representatives on legislation which serves the politician's local interests (a dam, highway, or establishing a military facility in their congressional district). Logrolling in practice which redistributes income towards specific regions or localities, does not, however, generally enhance efficiency. The end-result may include tariffs to protect individual industries or costly public works legislation. In such cases, logrolling on a national scale may be inefficient because legislators are trading purely local issues against national issues with fewer localised impacts.

Logrolling and rent-seeking strategies are facilitated by a lack of understanding by the general public of specific situations as well as of the institutions which allow such behaviour. It is rational for most voters to remain ignorant about the complexities of public policies because of the costs of becoming informed (see Part I, Chapters 1 and 2). Hence, the public choice argument on rational ignorance also applies.

Apologists for protection have succeeded in convincing many voters that the object of foreign trade is to export, and the imports in exchange are an unfortunate necessity. Those apologists emphasise the expansion of employment, or in some cases profits, as a result of increased exports. Defenders of protection also emphasise that imports cause unemployment. Politicians may thus find it easy to 'barter' competing interests and strike protectionist bargains that are advantageous to domestic business interests.

Responses to Protection

The outcome of the battle between home producers with a large potential gain from protection and unorganised consumers may also depend on predicting other nations' responses to protectionist policies, which involve the specific items to be protected and also the broader set of international trade issues flowing from the national and international restrictions on trade. Another government's response to protectionist initiatives will depend on what is economically advantageous to the country and the ability of special interests to counter those initiatives through government or international organisations such as the WTO. 'Tit-for-tat' rules that specify Nation B will respond to Nation A's trade restrictions by reciprocally imposing restrictions on Nation A's exports may dissuade Nation A from taking protectionist measures.

The effectiveness of such tit-for-tat rules in promoting general free trade is questionable at best. As a general rule, the economic theory (explanation) of international trade suggests that liberalising trade advances the country's economic interests without regard to whether the other country reciprocates. Tit-for-tat restrictions by one nation may tend to encourage others to adopt their own special restrictive rules, spawning a maze of regulatory impediments to international trade that can be invoked by rent-seeking domestic business groups to protect their favoured market positions. All individuals tend to be made better off with less restricted trade, and small economies are almost always better off if they impose no restrictions on trade, even if other nations follow an opposite course.

The discussion above indicates the potential complexity of both the technical issues of tit-for-tat as well as the importance of the political setting. In most cases consideration of the technical issues may seem only a rationalisation for straight-forward protection. It is difficult to judge many of these problems because they raise even more difficult technical questions. There is no obvious reason, for example, why an apple grower concerned about imported apples might not be interested in both the price of apples and also the possibility that his apple orchard will become infested with a disease brought in by imported apples.

The Costs of Protection and the Example of Agriculture

A key reason for the political successes of protection is that most people tend to consider only the immediate effects of protectionist policy on an industry group (or industry). The long-range impact of policy on society as a whole is largely ignored. This distorted vision occurs because of large, concentrated and easily identified beneficiaries (generally producers) and a large number of consumers each of whom experiences harm that is not large enough to justify the expense of opposition. Yet in total these harms outweigh the benefits to domestic producers. The distortion occurs even though consumers may be acutely aware of the damages due to protectionist policies.

Protection is common in agriculture. Arguments have often been made on the basis of protecting the income of farmers by reducing price fluctuations for traded commodities or simply to subsidise the development of the agricultural industry. 'Parity prices' are an example of agricultural protection in the United States. Under an agricultural parity price scheme, government artificially maintains prices at some outdated historical price ratio. The government may pursue a combination of purchasing surplus crops, withholding the product from the market, and inducing farmers to reduce acreage. All these approaches have one feature in common – they reduce supply and drive up prices. As long as demand is maintained, the price will rise due to the reduction in the available supply.

The European Union's Common Agricultural Policy (CAP) is another example of an institutional structure that allows the narrow beneficiaries of protection to maintain inefficient production policies which impose costs on a large number of people. The CAP began as an effort to guarantee high prices to European farmers by buying agricultural products in times when prices fell below specified levels. It also came to involve tariffs in order to prevent the inflow of foreign agricultural products by raising the price of imports to a level at which European production is much increased. Export subsidies were added to the mix. The CAP leads to major resource misallocations and imposes substantial costs (high prices) on European consumers.

Research has shown that the adverse effects of protection are not limited to wealthy industrial countries, but often occur in the impoverished Third World countries which can least afford them. Why is it that in rich countries, where farmers are a small minority, we generally find a heavily subsidised agricultural sector, while in poor countries, where farmers are in a majority, they are usually heavily taxed? According to Stanford economist Anne Krueger, until the 1980s most research on agricultural policy found that taxation of agriculture diminishes, and subsidisation eventually takes over, as countries become richer.[1] The puzzle is complicated in that the means by which farmers in rich countries are subsidised are very inefficient because income transfers are not arranged at least cost. Despite considerable research, there is so far no satisfactory resolution to this paradox. Nor are income distribution objectives accomplished through schemes based on supporting prices aimed at poor farmers: with smaller outputs small farmers receive smaller benefits and larger farmers larger benefits. While in both rich and poor countries employment and income transfers are often the avowed basis for government intervention, there is a high price to pay in resource transfers to less efficient users. In general, the protection of domestic agricultural producers redistributes income at the expense of the consumer and the tax-payer. As a consequence, prices of farm products within the EU are higher than they would be in the absence of protection.

The Progress Towards Free Trade
Despite the general agreement about the harmful consequences of protection, it can be expected to continue for the foreseeable future. The extent to which the move to liberalise trade will continue, thereby reducing the scope of these harmful consequences, will depend upon the ability of those who benefit from trade to organise and oppose particular protectionist policies. For example, software producers would benefit by decreasing tariffs on computers. The increase in demand for software would benefit them. Such 'positive sum' rent seekers (firms whose rent-seeking efforts are aimed at eliminating economically restrictive rules) may encourage

---

[1] A. O. Krueger, 'Political economy of agricultural policy', *Public Choice,* No. 87, 1996, pp. 163–75.

the movement towards free trade and spur the demise of protection, although on a gradual and piecemeal basis.

2

INTERNET GOVERNANCE

Introduction

AFTER DESCRIBING HOW THE INTERNET FUNCTIONS and providing a brief history, we discuss domestic (Federal Communications Commission (FCC)) and international (Internet Corporation for Assigned Names and Numbers (ICANN), World Intellectual Property Organization (WIPO)) institutions which will encourage rent seeking.

The effect of the regulations may be to slow down and possibly discourage the development of the Internet. It is, in particular, the board of directors of the new organisation, ICANN, which might undermine the activities of the other independent standard-setting bodies. There is also the risk that governments in Europe and elsewhere will see too many rents to ignore, and become more heavily involved in governance as a vehicle for income redistribution. A recent US FCC decision has opened the door to the imposition of access fees under the guise of universal service as the vehicle for wealth transfers from users in high-density areas (firms with inelastic demand and households) to users in low-density areas.

Public Choice Issues

The Internet has developed largely as a 'spontaneous order', without a central co-ordinating authority, in part because government regulators have failed to anticipate the pace of technology in this area, and thus have been slow to assert regulatory supervision. This chapter examines Internet governance from a public choice perspective, by noting the role of interest groups, politicians and bureaucrats in seeking to control rents and by pointing out the institutions which will influence the future development of this latest remarkable advance in communications technology.

Public choice theory holds that exercises of government power are driven by the material and ideological interests of politicians and bureaucrats and by the private parties who can reward them. Viewed through the lens of public choice theory, regulators are motivated to involve themselves in Internet governance not to promote consumer welfare, nor the efficiency yielded by competition, nor the additional economic surplus created by technological innovation. Rather, government intervention in the Internet, as in many other private arrangements, would be explained by the bureaucracy's interactions with four sets of interests:

(1) competitors of successful firms that want to hamstring their rivals or appropriate parts of their businesses;
(2) firms disadvantaged by technological change that seek to mitigate market outcomes unfavourable to them;
(3) the personal ambitions of government administrators who do not prosper in quiet times; and
(4) the class interest of the legal profession (trial lawyers) engaged in redistribution through lawsuits aimed at stifling market processes.

An Overview of Internet Governance

To understand Internet governance, it is useful to survey the technical structure and public and private contractual arrangements, as well as the public authorities through which the Internet is administered. The term 'network' is the key to the concept of the Internet governance. A computer network consists of two or more computers connected with cables or some other cellular link through which computers send information encoded as electrical impulses. Networks require that the computers they connect use the same network protocol. 'Internet' is a term coined by computer scientists for a network formed by connecting two or more networks together. The 'Internet' then refers to the series of small, local area networks (LANs) connected by several wide area networks (WANs). LANs are small networks privately owned by a single legal entity, such as a firm or a university, for its own benefit.

Every network functions by having all the computers attached to it recognise common network protocols ('top-level computer protocols' and 'Internet protocols', known as TCP/IP). It is the

TCP/IPs and the agreement of several network owners to use them that cement the Internet's many networks together into what appears to its users as a coherent, single entity. The time it takes for a message to travel across the Internet depends less on the Internet's physical geography than on the number of routers through which the message must travel. Messages and comments are broken up at their point of origin into 'packets', each with its own address and routing instructions. They are transmitted over connecting networks (WANs) for reassembly at their destination. Specialised computers select the least congested route for transmitting the packets, which may take very different paths, passing through many networks and being routed onwards at each location. Another computer will reassemble the messages based on self-contained instructions. Neither the sender nor the receiver will know or care which routes the message may have travelled. It is this packet-switching technology which enables the information to be sent without regard to tracking or monitoring, but it is the *tracking over different networks to end-users* which will enable public and private interest parties to engage in rent seeking.

The Internet involves a set of hardware and software relationships which connect entities around the world. The networks which comprise the Internet operate with one another because of the common TCP/IP protocols and also because of the series of contracts among the entities that own the cabling. Access by end-users to the Internet is generally provided by Internet Service Providers (ISPs) or Online Service Providers (OSPs), although many large firms may maintain their own direct connection to the Internet. ISPs are engaged primarily in the sale of Internet access to business and consumers. OSPs, such as American Online, Compu-serve or Prodigy, offer their own proprietary content as well as access to the Internet. Any attempt by government to administer, and hence regulate and tax the network as a single entity invariably encounters the problem of persuading many individual network owners and system programmers to agree on one standard.

The administration of the Internet's mail system is based on the Internet Protocol address. Here, at the end point, is a convenient place for regulators (domestic and foreign) to add a tax or allow a regulated entity to capture a rent. For the mail system to function, every computer sending and receiving information must have a unique number, so that the network routers can know where to send each packet of information and computers on the Internet can know which packets are intended for them. The High-Performance Computing and Communications Division of the Information Sciences Institute (ISI) operates the IANA (Internet Assigned Numbers Authority) as an unincorporated entity. The network addresses provide each computer on a network with a unique identifier in the form of numbers. Before a computer can use a domain name to contact another computer on the Internet, it must translate the domain name into the IP address to which it corresponds.

The assignment of numbers permits authorities to discriminate and thus creates the potential for rent seeking – rather like the zoning of commercial and residential activities. Consider, for example, the distinction between a .com and an .org which engages in substantial commercial activities. A non-profit environmental group, such as the Sierra Club, or the American Association for Retired Persons (AARP) has the .org designation even though a substantial part of its income is generated by the sale of goods and services. People may have a more favourable view of purchasing products and services from an .org than buying similar goods from a .com, which they perceive as a purely for-profit organisation. One would expect entrepreneurs operating commercial activities to appreciate this distinction between an .org and a .com and to be willing to invest resources to acquire the valued .org designation. One would also expect those responsible for designating names and numbers to understand this and to seek to capture at least some of the available rents through devices such as price discrimination and bribes.

Network Solutions, Inc. (NSI) operates the authoritative server for the generic TLDs (Top Level Domains) known as .com, .org, and .net. Other institutions, including the US government and certain foreign entities, are responsible for assigning addresses for other TLDs. The US government registers addresses for the .gov TLD, and foreign entities (under the control of their governments) register TLDs that are hosted within their territories. These in turn are reached through the use of nation-specific address labels, such as .uk for the United Kingdom and .fr for France.

Significantly, the TCP/IP standards that allow the Internet to function are developed by consensus through a private voluntary standards-setting mechanism co-ordinated by the Internet Engineering Task Force (IETF). The IETF up to now has been open to all comers and has operated without government interference. Whether this crucial state of affairs – a free market – will continue is uncertain. There are increasing signs that politicians and regulators may seek more involvement in Internet governance by intervening in the developing structure of property rights.

A Brief History of the Internet

The Internet owes its creation to US Government subsidies. Approximately 30 years ago, the Defence Advanced Research Projects Agency (DARPA) funded an electronic computer network among scientists, aimed at facilitating the exchange of research, which was transformed into ARPANET. IANA (the Internet Assigned Numbers Authority discussed above) was assigned the exclusive task of assigning unique numerical identifiers (addresses) to facilitate communication among network participants. Eventually DARPA transferred its funding and administration of non-national security-related government-supported networks to the National Science Foundation (NSF), developed its own NSFNET, and worked with federal agencies and the private sector in the development of networking technologies.

In 1992, Congress enacted legislation which gave the NSF authority to commercialise the NSFNET, in a manner that would be consistent with the creation of benefits for NSF's research and educational activities. Significantly, the NSF encouraged the development of this new commercialised network, newly dubbed the Internet, by transforming the NSFNET into a series of autonomous networks. The decentralised nature of the NSFNET allowed for experimentation with a variety of institutional arrangements (including some reliance on privatisation and commercialisation) on an *ad hoc* basis. In turn, as the operation of individual networks grew, network services and applications attracted users beyond the core research and education communities. In 1995, the NSF ceased funding the NSFNET infrastructure, which had provided high speed connectivity among regional networks. Instead the NSF provided support for four network access points, which facilitated interconnection among regional research and education networks and the growing number of commercial networks. This development had the effect of privatising the basic network infrastructure, while maintaining open interconnection practices and drawing competing providers to the market for Internet services.

The NSF, in co-operation with the Federal Networking Council (representing network users in the different federal government agencies), assumed the lead in funding basic Internet information services, including domain name and network number registration. In 1992, the NSF contracted with Network Solutions, Inc. (NSI), a Virginia-based company, for five years to manage the registration of domain names (.com, .org, and .net) and their IP numbers.[1] In addition, DARPA, on behalf of the Federal Networking Council, entered into a contract assigning the functions of the IANA to a group of computer scientists headed by Dr Jonathan Postel at the University of Southern California's Information Sciences Institute (ISI).[2] The functions of ISI have included the oversight of the domain name system, the oversight of network numbering, and delegation to other entities of the authority to operate particular country code TLDs. In June 1997, NSF and NSI agreed to separate the management of network numbers from other management activities under their contract. Number registration for users in the Americas is now assigned to the new American Registry for Internet Numbers (ARIN). In turn, ARIN's assignment of network numbers was made

---

[1] To date, NSI has assigned some three million addresses, charging $70 for each. In 1998, NSI registered about 1.9 million new domain names, nearly double its 1997 total of 960,000 names. This monopoly has allowed it to realise phenomenal growth in revenue and profits. Its net income for the first nine months of 1998 grew threefold, to $7.5 million, or 45 cents per share, compared with $2.5 million, or 20 cents per share, for the first nine months of 1997. On 5 January 1999, NSI announced plans for both a stock split and a secondary offering of 4.5 million shares. In December 1998, NSI's stock had tripled to an all-time high of $172.25 after it announced alliances with the Netscape Communications Corp. and Yahoo.

[2] Dr Postel died in November 1998.

subject to the oversight of the IANA. Through these arrangements, the US Government affects the operation of half of the world's root servers, the master computers that keep track of domain names and co-ordinate Internet traffic.

In 1997, the US Government developed a regulatory proposal on Internet policy (a 'green paper'). It called for a transition to competition in domain name assignments, and a phasing out of the government's responsibilities *vis-à-vis* the Internet, although retaining residual authority to intervene if anti-trust or other Internet-related public policy problems should arise. In order to accomplish these ends (competition in domain names and phasing out of the government-bestowed monopoly), US government representatives discussed the Green Paper with US and foreign interest groups. Two key actions were taken. *First*, it was decided that the NSI's monopoly in the TLDs under its control should be phased out. *Second*, a new, private, non-profit corporation was to be created, to take over responsibility for the oversight of Internet numbering, to assume oversight over the TLD system (including the authority to establish new TLDs), and to assume other (not clearly specified) Internet management functions. The Commerce Department was assigned the task of entering into a co-operative agreement with this new company on behalf of the US Government. In the fall of 1998, the Commerce Department published a *Federal Register* announcement soliciting proposals for this role of a new company. A new entity calling itself the Internet Company for Assigned Names and Numbering (ICANN), which in significant part was comprised of IANA personnel, was selected to fulfil this role. In response to foreign concerns, ICANN's Board is required to include representatives from Europe and Asia and to hold meetings open to the public and to emphasise 'transparent' decision-making. Supporting organisations – interest groups whose members are involved in Internet-related activities – will advise ICANN's Board. In addition, the World Intellectual Property Organisation (WIPO), which is dedicated to promoting strong trademark and copyright protection, will provide advice to ICANN.

The Commerce Department, which had assumed authority from the NSF for the government's co-operative agreement with NSI, renegotiated a two-year agreement with NSI which extends its monopoly to the end of September 2001. Under the terms of the new agreement, NSI is developing software which will be licensed to other firms that wish to compete in domain name registration. NSI's monopoly rents are thus retained through licensing. It is envisaged that competition among registrars – the parties that register domain names and maintain registers of individual top level domain names, such as .com – will result from this development. This new arrangement may also help defuse anti-trust suits brought against NSI, on the ground that it had illegally monopolised domain name registration. In the spring of 1999, NSI began to work with ICANN to test the new software with four firms that were given limited registration authority on an experimental basis.[3]

What Future for the Internet?

The Internet is under siege from those who seek to use government regulation – telecommunications regulators, tax authorities, and ICANN, to name just three bodies. We have already seen that, in response to overseas pressure, ICANN's Board of Directors includes foreign representatives, and that ICANN has 'transparent' decision-making processes that allow for public input. While we can expect the usual array of consumer advocacy groups which argue for lower prices, others will argue for special privileges and subsidies. Educational interest groups and telephone companies have been successful in obtaining such subsidies.

First, Internet Service Providers (ISPs) have not up to now paid to gain access to local phone lines controlled by incumbent local exchange carriers (ILECs), such as Bell Atlantic. This exclusion may eventually change in the light of a February 1999 Federal

---

[3] Once the new registrars are permanent, NSI will be obligated to transfer registrations of addresses ending in .com, .net and .org to its competitors if customers decide they would rather deal with one of the new companies. Many analysts anticipate, however, that NSI will maintain its dominance, in part because the process for moving the Internet governance to the private sector and opening the registration business has taken so long, giving the company much-needed time to diversify and solidify its leadership.

Communications Commission (FCC) ruling. Even if one accepts the argument that ISPs should bear the congestion costs they impose on phone networks, there remains the risk that, once involved with the Internet, the FCC will have an incentive to expand its involvement, given rapid growth and the wealth created by the Internet. This argument stems from public choice: bureaucrats have the incentive to aggrandise their status and increase their budgets by expanding their regulatory scope to encompass new powers, particularly when they create wealth. Public choice suggests that bureaucrats may seek to redistribute wealth from newly regulated sectors to satisfy special-interest constituencies – such as 'public interest' groups that want to expand the scope of 'universal service' or the politically well-represented rural users that want to garner even larger subsidies. The FCC has engaged in rent redistribution in the past and, as the wealth associated with the Internet grows, the FCC would likely undertake this sort of intervention.

Second, the Internet also faces the threat that individual states and foreign governments, seeking new tax revenues to provide desired benefits to rent-seeking recipients of government largesse, will seek to tax Internet transmissions or the instrumentalities through which Internet services are provided. Two alternative plausible ways to tax Internet transactions would be either a tax based on all calls to an area code designated solely for Internet access or a tax on the volume of traffic through each ISP. As we have mentioned above, one might envisage discriminatory treatment in favour of all calls placed to .org websites. The value of such designations would increase and lead to the expenditure of resources to acquire this privilege and those organisations which provide such designations (like ICANN and NSI) would benefit.

In the US, the Internet Tax Freedom Act of 1998 established a moratorium on Internet taxation by government authorities at every level until October 2000, and it may well be extended. No such moratorium applies to foreign governments. Taxation would slow the growth of the Internet, and may affect investment decisions, the organisation of firms, and thus the structure of Internet governance. Furthermore, we would expect that those countries which tax

Internet-related activities least will experience the fastest growth of Internet commerce and the facilities that sustain it.

Third, another major threat to the Internet's growth may come from ICANN. Its Board members, representing constituencies which would be expected to engage in rent seeking, might, for example, want to restrict the growth of Internet top-level domain names as a way of maintaining their monopoly rents. The incentive of interest groups ranges from simply holding down the number of websites to denying the registration of similar website addresses. Conceivably ICANN's Board may find it more effective to enlist government to limit the number of domain names and provide restrictive criteria for authorising new names. This would enable them to collect the rents generated by their monopoly status while avoiding the charge that their actions were somehow self-serving. The unfortunate consequence would be to constrain the growth of new competitive opportunities that would otherwise be spawned by new top-level domains which might even include new parallel Internet systems. By centralising the authority for top-level domain names, government would create the circumstances in which rent seeking may flourish.

Conclusion

There are, however, forces that may operate against efforts by ICANN to regulate the Internet. Standards-setting bodies as well as technology providers might be expected to engage in positive-sum rent-seeking[4] efforts to convince governments that such meddling, whether inspired by ICANN or other constituency interests, would be wealth destructive and counterproductive. Moreover, the possibility of creating valuable intellectual property rights through new top level domains which amount to new parallel Internets would encourage possible owners of such rights to resist.

It is clear that public choice analysis provides a useful framework and valuable insights with which to understand many aspects of Internet governance, past, present, and prospective, and thus the

---

[4] A. F. Abbott and G. L. Brady, 'Welfare Gains from Innovation-Induced Rent Seeking', *Cato Journal*, Vol. 10, No. 5, Fall 1991, pp. 63–74.

advantages and disadvantages of proposed policy options. Continued research along these lines is warranted as technological progress unfolds and further political regulation is proposed.

APPLYING PUBLIC CHOICE

TO TELECOMMUNICATIONS

THIS CHAPTER USES RENT-SEEKING ANALYSIS to examine the prospects for liberalising telecommunications. While focussing on US regulation, it also takes account of developments that are spurring international competition and hence political pressures for a market-oriented telecommunications policy. Pressures from abroad and technical change are having the fortuitous consequence of overwhelming the national regulatory institutions in many areas of telecommunications policy. Public choice analysis provides important insights about the political and institutional forces that limit deregulation and the prospects for cost-reducing innovations to be passed on to consumers.

Overview

Telecommunications is characterised by rapid technological development and expanding markets despite complex regulation and intense rent-seeking activity. It provides a telling example of the power of the US Congress and regulatory bureaucracies to bestow rents on politicians and interest groups.

The Telecommunications Act of 1996 (the '1996 Act'), the major law governing US telecommunications, has liberalisation as its ostensible goal. The notion that consumers should have the choice to purchase the most efficient telecommunications services supplier, whether domestic or foreign, is straightforward, and should be reasonably simple to implement by breaking down impediments to consumer choice. But, due to the actions of bureaucrats, politicians, and agents of special interests, progress has been slow.

The 1996 Act retains a panoply of short-run regulatory limitations on the activities of new and incumbent firms; it mandates numerous new federal and federal-state regulatory proceedings; and it includes a host of special 'universal service' subsidies for favoured groups based on income and cost of service. Such provisions reflect the political agreements designed to attract broad-based financial support from diverse firms having conflicting interests and electoral support from politically active 'public-interest' lobbies.

In particular, the 1996 Act offers the regulatory agency, the Federal Communications Commission (FCC), additional opportunities to 'micro-manage', since it is required to undertake major new rule-making proceedings in several activities. The *first* is interconnection charges, which local operating companies are authorised to require from long-distance companies to administer their toll calls. The *second* is universal service, which involves a system of fees that telephone companies are assessed (and charge their customers) to subsidise telephone service for low-income and rural consumers. While provisions of the Act delayed regulatory reform, rapid technological change and burgeoning international competition for telecommunications investment cannot be thwarted in the long run.

As a consequence of market liberalisation, it is expected that telecommunications prices will fall, the variety of services will broaden, and new technologies will be developed. The US political and institutional structure, however, has retarded liberalisation. *First*, complex regulations separating the telephone, cable, and radio and television broadcasting sectors have prevented the electromagnetic spectrum from being allocated to the highest-valued uses. *Second*, regulatory barriers to entry for firms with compatible services (cable television, electric utilities) have deterred the introduction of new cost-saving technologies. Although technological advance has continued to erode the position of entrenched interests, technology alone is unlikely to offset completely the effects of regulation in order to produce the immense cost savings in telecommunications that would be feasible in the absence of political impediments. Clearly, such institutions are critical in bringing about regulatory reform. Public choice insights into rent seeking, logrolling, and bureaucracy may aid policy-makers by identifying potential bottlenecks and enabling them to evaluate competing institutional structures. Moreover, an informed electorate will be more sceptical of the motivation of legislators and bureaucrats.

Reform: Regulatory Costs, Innovation, and Privatisation – The Forces From Abroad

According to one assessment, the Telecommunications Act of 1996 will provide a 70 per cent reduction in telecommunications prices for Americans by 2005. This reduction will stem from scaling back regulatory constraints on competition – constraints which have engendered substantial delays in approving technology and resulting welfare losses. Since 1991, for example, the FCC has held back the commercialisation of a form of wireless cable (called Local Multi-point Distribution System) on the basis that the FCC requires more time to formulate licensing and other regulations for the technology. It delayed by up to four years (1989–93) efforts by telephone companies to build and operate video dial tone networks, a competitive alternative to cable television. This is now moot since the 1996 Act allows telephone companies to have a financial interest in cable. It took the FCC five years (1990–95) to start licensing the new, less expensive form of cellular technology, 'personal communications services'.

Huber and Thorne[1] estimate the costs of telecommunications licensing procedures alone at $600 million annually. They estimate the costs of this process at over four times the size of the FCC's relatively modest budget of $158 million which has spawned a cadre of 2,300 lawyers in the communications bar receiving fees averaging over $200,000 per lawyer per year. Estimates of the redistribution to the communications bar is a far more impressive figure, but deceptively low at $460 million per year. In return, this $460 million per year generates process costs of up to $140 million per year, not to mention tens of millions of dollars in congressional contributions and lobbyists' fees. These estimates of the redistribution do not fully

---

[1] P. W. Huber and J. Thorne, 'Economic Licencing Reform' (unpublished manuscript, March 1996). This paper is based on a presentation on 17 January 1996 to the American Enterprise Institute Conference on Revising Regulatory Reform.

reflect the cost since many of these lawyers and lobbyists could be engaged in productive activities.

Dwarfing direct expenditures, however, is the impact of tele-communications lawyers, lobbyists, and consultants on innovation through regulatory delay. These costs are likely to be hundreds of billions of dollars per year. Regulatory delays and barriers to competition alone are estimated to have reduced GDP by $300 billion per year in 1995.

An obvious explanation of such costs is rent seeking, but there is more to the story. The bureaucracy, the telecommunications bar, and parts of the telecommunications industry have the incentive to invest in the creation and maintenance of rents through complex regulation which serves as the avenue for future rent seeking. There are several factors, however, which have eroded the ability of regulators to maintain the rent structure. Rapid technological developments in the telecommunications industry, coupled with the trend towards increased privatisation of state telecommunications monopolies around the world (discussed below), the growth in support for spectrum auctions, and an emerging consensus supportive of competition have limited the ability of regulators to protect and expand rents.

Impediments to Liberalisation: Logrolling and Rent Seeking in the Legislatures

As we have seen, despite the global changes in the international telecommunications market, the FCC remains a prime target of rent seeking. It retains the ability to bestow, deny, or re-allocate rents among private parties through regulatory decisions and thus affect the value of property rights in the telecommunications industry. Its portfolio of monopoly powers which engender rent seeking include setting rates, granting licences, and other powers that govern the nature of competition among the firms. In addition to the FCC, Congress and executive agencies (such as the Commerce Department's National Telecommunications and Information Administration (NTIA) and the Justice Department's Antitrust Division) develop legislative and regulatory 'norms' and thus invite rent-seeking activities. Rent-seeking efforts also target the state public utility commissions, which regulate intra-state telephone rates.

Protection of Domestic Rents from Foreign Competition
The protection of domestic companies from foreign competition also bestowed by the FCC, is a valuable special privilege which encourages investment in rent seeking. Dominant firms lobby to limit potential competition within their sectors and to block the intrusion of foreign competitors. The Federal Communications Act of 1934 has been construed as limiting foreign firms to a 25 per cent stake in US telecommunications firms. Because larger investments require FCC approval, both domestic and foreign firms have the incentive to lobby the FCC for decisions in their favour. The FCC's ability to protect domestic telecommunications firms from foreign competition will continue to have a profound effect on the ability of the consumer to obtain the benefits of reform. But there is yet more to the rent seeking story.

Restrictions on Facilities and Spectrum Use
Notwithstanding the ostensible legislative intent of the 1996 Act to liberalise markets, intra-state carriers such as local telephone service suppliers may not construct new facilities or discontinue service without advance permission from the FCC. An additional impediment to market liberalisation is the FCC's requirement that parts of the electromagnetic spectrum be devoted exclusively to designated services (such as television or cellular telephony). This restriction prevents entrepreneurs from purchasing spectrum licences for particular purposes (UHF television), and employing their licences for higher-valued purposes (cellular telephony). Both telephone companies and broadcasters must receive FCC approval before they can embark on any new use or change an existing use of the electromagnetic spectrum. The lengthy regulatory hearings require the employment of expensive telecommunications lawyers whose services are demanded by the regulated firms, the new entrants and the bureaucracy, all of whom seek to obtain interpretations in their own interest.

Furthermore, in the US, a large portion of the electromagnetic spectrum cannot be traded in the market because it is assigned to federal government agencies (for example, the NTIA and the FCC). In short, unlike the scarce resources in most other industries, free competition is not permitted in telecommunications. While auctions of limited amounts of spectrum (including former federally-used wavelengths) have been allowed in recent years, such auctions require that the spectrum made available be put to specific pre-designated uses which of itself would tend to lower the price paid for the wavelengths. Because the amount of spectrum released has been – and will continue to be – small, artificially high prices have been established (thereby creating billions of dollars in federal auction fee revenues).

Managing Competition with Traditional Telephony –
Preserving Rents
Cable television companies have long been touted as potential competitors to traditional telephone companies, but their incentive and ability to compete in telephony have been stymied by regulatory enactments. The 1992 enactment of cable industry 're-regulation' occurred after extensive rent-seeking activity by numerous parties. The legislation passed despite President Bush's veto, and created new opportunities for rent seeking by cable and non-cable firms. Cable companies and their rivals ('direct broadcast satellite' firms and wireless cable microwave firms) appear before the FCC and local regulatory bodies in order to influence the regulations. Cable industry spokesmen often claim that tight regulatory constraints will deter cable industry investment and thereby undermine the introduction of new services and new programming to the detriment of consumers. In particular, the FCC established rules that require cable operators to provide competitors with access to their programming, although this had been overturned by the 1996 Act. This provision encourages litigation by cable operators to prevent access and by firms seeking to capture rents from cable access. Regardless of whether such rules deter economically-efficient arrangements (such as vertical integration and exclusivity agreements), as critics charge, or instead have the effect of advancing competition through programme access for cable firms' rivals, as proponents claim, the

113

end-result is extensive rent seeking. Key members of Congress involved in the supervision of cable technology through cable regulation oversight hearings may be viewed as intermediaries in the rent distribution process; they will of course continue to be lobbied and act as brokers for rent transfers.

Universal Service: Political Logrolling in Action

Even as limited regulatory reforms gradually open markets, regional politics will continue to play a role in telecommunications. Logrolling explains the redistribution from low-cost high-density urban customers to high-cost low-density rural users through universal service provisions. Formalised in the 1982 AT&T consent decree, access charges are transfer payments from long-distance companies to local companies designed to continue the politically popular below-cost pricing of basic local service. The FCC and the state regulatory bodies control the magnitude and nature of subsidies implemented through below-cost pricing for consumers of local telephone service, rural residents, and the poor.

Universal service is one of the most important, contentious, and poorly understood issues of US telecommunications liberalisation. Its role as a vehicle for income transfers has been expanded in the 1996 Act. Public choice analysis helps explain the emergence of universal service as a major policy issue. Universal service entails both direct and indirect subsidies which maintain basic residential service at rates deemed 'affordable' by regulatory authorities. Subsidised access is limited to basic telephony and emergency services for individual consumers, with some states offering subsidies to schools and other state institutions. Universal service also has important implications for international competitiveness, the development of new technology, and investment decisions.

The concept of 'universal service' dates back to 1907 as part of the marketing strategy of the Bell System (AT&T) to exploit business customers in the dense and lucrative urban markets. The growth strategy of the Bell system sought to build upon the benefits of a single, unified service for urban and rural areas. AT&T sought to suppress competition by the independent suppliers of telephone service. State regulators saw benefits through centralisation of control flowing from the elimination of such competition. Universal service fitted well with these political forces because it was tied to monopoly control of the system by Bell and the regulators.

AT&T publicly argued for regulated local exchange monopolies on the grounds of fragmentation and lack of centralisation in existing telephone service. This position was quite different from the egalitarian argument that telephone services should be 'more' affordable. Gradually, through the late 1920s, with the approval of regulators, the politically powerful Bell system absorbed many of its competitors and offered interconnection to systems with which it did not compete. By the time the FCC and the federal regulatory apparatus were consolidated by the Federal Communications Act of 1934, regulation had replaced competition as the preferred method to restrain prices.

The regulations which evolved into the modern concept of universal service as a transfer appeared in the late 1930s. Based on the US Supreme Court's decision in *Smith v. Illinois Bell*, regulators began to allocate certain fixed costs associated with the connection to the network local and long-distance categories. The argument was that because both long-distance and local calls were made through the same facilities, the cost of these facilities should be apportioned between long-distance and local service. This marked the beginning of the complex system of cross-subsidies which came to serve as a primary impediment to liberalisation.

Residential telephone use expanded rapidly in the 1940s and 1950s and with it came increasingly complex regulation. Regulators began to favour price discrimination between residential users and business users. Shifting the costs of local service to long-distance services provided a means to keep retail rates for local service low. It is easy to understand why this separation occurred. State regulators were politically motivated to be seen to do a good job by providing low rates to 'local' users, who voted for the people who appointed them. Decreasing charges for telephone service increased the number of users and thus the rents accruing to legislators. Costs were shifted to business users, who were seen as better able to afford the higher rates than households. In essence, households voted for business to transfer income to them through lower phone rates.

The AT&T monopoly made it simple for the regulators to produce these subsidies. Since the costs were not actually transferred among different companies, the transfers were essentially hidden. However, major changes occurred with the development of microwave technology and the entrepreneurship of Microwave Communications Incorporated (MCI) in the early 1970s. MCI developed a competitive long-distance company that began by focusing on business customers. Their efforts involved breaking down regulatory impediments to innovation and competition. This process had the effect of creating a regulatory lag, in which long-distance rates were kept above economic costs, and prices were prevented from falling as rapidly as technological advancements would allow. Rents were protected by FCC rules aimed at slowing down the introduction of cost-decreasing technology by innovative firms such as MCI. That MCI grew rapidly after gaining this foothold reflected the distortions inherent in the cost-allocation practices used to support local subsidies.

After the AT&T divestiture in 1982, in which AT&T's 'local' operations were 'spun off' to separate regional Bell operating companies (RBOCs), universal service subsidies were maintained by a régime of 'access charges' paid by long-distance companies to the RBOCs for access to local telephone exchanges. The 1996 Act further encouraged rent seeking by introducing a new form of universal service. With Vice President Gore in the forefront, the Clinton Administration sought to extend the subsidy, arguing that this was needed to avoid a society divided into information 'haves' and 'have-nots' (the 'digital divide'). Specifically, the Administration sought to subsidise service to assure 'affordable service to all Americans, including every classroom in every school, every library, and every rural health care facility'.[2] As public choice theory would lead us to expect, Congress sought to extend the services deemed universal and to expand the groups that benefit from them. Not surprisingly, the expanded universal service plan was enthusiastically supported by

---

[2] R. E. Hunt, 'Implementation of the Telecommunication Act of 1996', before the Subcommittee on Telecommunications and Finance, Committee on Commerce, US House of Representatives, 18 July 1996, pp. 16–17.

members of Congress from largely rural states and by educational institutions.

With the move towards competition in all telecommunications markets, the excessive access charges some firms pay will disappear. In the future, a wider variety of firms will be required to pay access charges in order to 'level' the competitive playing field and to maintain the feasibility of continued transfer payments through this mechanism.

Universal Service and Economic Efficiency

Imposing 'universal service' charges on all suppliers of interstate telecommunications services, as required by the 1996 Act, is at odds with economic efficiency. If they are to be subsidised, services for the poor and for rural residents are more efficiently financed through general tax levies and transfer payments (negative income tax, income tax credits or even 'telecommunications stamps' for low-income people). As previously discussed, rent seeking explains the bargaining which brought the current subsidies régime about and keeps the regulations in place. Continuing to use telecommunications companies as vehicles for such payments, of course, has the political advantage for Congress of disguising the true costs of the subsidies. Moreover, the 1996 Act specifies that the FCC is to decide on an ongoing basis – and in the light of new technologies – what services constitute the 'universal service' bundle. This gives 'public interest' groups an incentive to lobby and litigate to broaden the set of services that favoured groups will receive.

There are additional pay-offs to interest groups as well as direct benefits to telephone users. Interest groups use their participation to advertise for contributions to continue their lobbying activities. These groups will undoubtedly argue that 'fairness' requires poor and rural consumers be given more low-cost access to the 'information highway', so as not to create a society of the 'information rich' and the 'information poor'. In turn, as part of the exchange, the FCC may use universal service proceedings to maintain regulatory control over the full array of telecommunications service providers and to recognise favoured public-interest groups.

To its credit, the 1996 Act does make more explicit the Byzantine set of pre-existing accounting and implicit subsidies through which universal service payments are financed. However, FCC proceedings mandated by the 1996 Act, such as decisions on the access charge and universal service policies described above, may also generate legal challenges and attendant delay, depending upon the approach pursued by the FCC and the parties affected by those proceedings.

Freeing up the Spectrum: The Obstacles to Reform
Although reliance on auctions to allocate the spectrum for new telecommunications uses will increase, most of the spectrum will remain subject to pre-existing administrative allocations – by the FCC for private users and by the NTIA for federal government users. FCC regulation will continue to prevent current users from migrating to new uses (for example, from UHF broadcast television to mobile telephony or paging) and existing federal governmental uses will largely remain in place with only a gradual transfer of spectrum from federal to private users. In the long run, it will be new technology and new uses of the spectrum (whether accomplished through legislation, litigation, technological innovation, or a combination of all three) that will break down the most insurmountable barriers to competition in the communications and information industries. Market forces will bring about changes that politicians and interest groups cannot prevent. Systemic changes will fall into place as technology renders existing rules obsolete. The windfall rents that arose from FCC lotteries for cellular telephone licences will be largely avoided in the future, thanks to the passage of legislation in 1993 (as part of the Clinton Administration's budget package) providing for the auctioning off of some NTIA spectrum currently held for federal government use.

Portions of this auctioned off spectrum are being dedicated to 'broad-band' PCS communications services (advanced telephone and wireless services), to 'narrow-band' advanced paging and wireless services and to Interactive Video Data Services (IVDS) (interactive television services such as surveys or home banking). Auctions for 10 nation-wide 'narrow-band' spectrum licences in July 1994 raised over $230 million for the government, far more than had generally been expected. Six hundred IVDS licences were auctioned for over $80 million in July 1994. By using spectrum auctions, first proposed by Professor Ronald Coase in 1959, the federal government hopes to capture the expected revenues associated with anticipated rents deriving from spectrum use.[3]

Nevertheless, as indicated above, firms 'trapped' in existing uses – and those that desire pre-licensed wavelengths for new uses – will have to utilise the federal regulatory process in order to change the *status quo*. This, of course, will entail rent seeking, whether through lobbying and actions before administrative agencies or attempts to obtain favourable legislation. If this rent seeking were directed merely at securing narrow licences for individual interests, it would reduce general welfare. If, however, a broader rent-seeking campaign succeeded in eliminating the existing 'zoning' of the spectrum – that is, eliminating regulatory barriers to new uses of spectrum allocations – welfare would rise, because the welfare gains (new market opportunities) from 'freeing up' the spectrum would in all likelihood greatly outweigh the costs of the rent-seeking campaign.

Liberalising Telecommunications: Will Competitive Forces More than Offset the Working of the Regulatory Process?
New technologies and resultant competitive pressures, spurred by privatisation, are reducing the ability of industries to affect regulatory policy to their own advantage. Following the lead of British Telecommunications (BT), which was privatised in 1984, other European nations and developing nations are privatising state telecom monopolies. Leaders in deregulation include Chile (1982), New Zealand (1989), Australia (1991), and Guatemala (1996). In addition to revenue the government receives from selling shares, and the generally undervalued capital obtained by the subscribers, privatisation is driven by the general realisation that the privately owned telecommunications sector is more innovative.

---

[3] R. H. Coase, 'The Federal Communications Commission', *Journal of Law and Economics*, Vol. 2, 1959.

Privatisation reduces the ability of telecom suppliers to charge high prices, thereby lowering the costs (and enhancing the international competitive prospects) of domestic industries that rely heavily on telecom services. Further efficiencies are obtained because once privatisation occurs, the former state monopolies have an incentive to shift their activities out of areas covered by rigid regulations, including the accounting and settlements rules that govern the prices national carriers charge foreign carriers for international phone calls. These prices traditionally have been set well above cost, an unsustainable situation in a competitive environment.

The increasing ability of businesses and some consumers to employ new technologies and communicate through means not covered by the accounting and settlements rules is beginning to erode existing inefficient arrangements. For example, Reuters News Service has its own internal communications system which bypasses the regulated common carriers. Furthermore, 'call back' services, which scan to select the lowest cost line, utilise computers to shift telephone traffic to countries that maintain lower international long-distance prices, thereby undermining accounting and settlements rules. The growth of the Internet and Internet software which facilitates voice as well as data transmissions not covered by these rules is also important in this regard.

Liberalisation is being promoted by supranational institutions seeking economic integration. For example, free trade in such services as telecommunications between European Union nations is one of the central points of the Maastricht Treaty of 1992.

Such developments helped spur over 70 countries to enter into a 'Basic Telecommunications Services' agreement under the auspices of the World Trade Organisation in 1997. Under this agreement, the signatories have committed themselves to open basic telephone service to foreign competition. Foreign entrants will be accorded 'most favoured nation' status which is to say there will be no discrimination against foreign firms. Aware of these developments, the International Telecommunications Union (a UN organisation with over 170 signatories) is encouraging developing countries to lower charges towards cost and to make up revenues lost thereby through the introduction of competitive régimes that encourage foreign investment.

Concluding Comments

As we have seen, competition, whether accomplished through legislation, litigation, technological innovation, or a combination of all three, may be expected to break down the most significant barriers to competition in the communications and information industries in the long run. Breaking down regulatory barriers will spur innovation and improve resource allocation in the telecoms industry (and in industries highly dependent upon telecom), both domestically and internationally. The rapid development of telecoms deregulation overseas may also spur regulatory change in the US, as domestic firms seek additional flexibility in order to compete with foreign competition.

Public choice adds much to our understanding of the forces which are bringing about liberalisation in telecom markets. The theory of rent seeking provides important insights into obstacles and impediments to the liberalisation of the telecom market and useful understanding of the role of institutions in bringing about reforms. It also addresses the factors affecting the manner and rate of change.

4

APPLYING PUBLIC CHOICE

TO ENVIRONMENTAL POLICY

ENVIRONMENTAL QUALITY IS THE CLASSIC EXAMPLE OF A 'PUBLIC GOOD' that, once provided, everyone receives regardless of their willingness to pay and without reducing the amount others may consume. Environmental quality management takes the form of preventing or remedying damage. Some external effects which cause environmental harms result from private actions. They may be caused by illegal actions such as dumping of toxic materials or discharge of air pollutants, or by actions allowable by government rules with unanticipated third party effects. They may also result from government policies, such as excessive irrigation encouraged by subsidies, overgrazing of federal lands, or inadequate control of federal activities such as electric power generation or weapons production and testing.

Historically, the common law doctrines of nuisance and trespass provided remedies for the damage to private property. In the US after 1970, major environmental laws replaced common law remedies with complex regulations driven by technology-based 'command and control'. With few exceptions, the US management of air and water quality limits the response of business firms to 'add on' controls at the end of the production process rather than to encourage production technologies that cost-effectively reduce the byproducts which cause environmental damage. The government's approach is based on technology in existence and not directly tied to the action necessary to reach the air quality standards. There are provisions in the Clean Air Act which allow trading of pollution permits, but these are grounded in technological requirements for the Best Available Technology (BAT) discussed in this chapter. Indoor air quality is maintained by control of emissions from appliances such as heaters and 'secondhand' tobacco smoke.

Public Choice and the Clean Air Act

Public choice analysis explains Clean Air Act regulations, how they arose, and why they are difficult to change. Reflecting the decisions and interaction of numerous individuals (scientists, politicians, environmentalists, bureaucrats) and special-interest groups, environmental policy is a process which incorporates economic, legal, social, and political considerations.

For many environmental issues, the policy debate is characterised by two perspectives. The *first* group, the environmentalists, demands not only chemically pure air and water but requires uniform control for all dischargers in all regions even when not necessary to achieve this goal. A *second* group, the free-market environmentalists, favours the allocation of resources on the basis of market-driven values. They view the outdoor air as a valuable resource for efficient disposal of pollutants based on the 'carrying capacity' of the air or its ability to neutralise pollutants. The environmentalists' symbols are dramatic and designed to capture the moral high ground. Their images evoke the argument that industrial firms are base and greedy despoilers who threaten the moral order of society.

Strange Bedfellows: Bootleggers and Baptists

While the special-interest suppliers of products and services which affect the environment have sufficiently similar interests to form lobbying groups seeking legislative action, change in environmental policy may also be influenced by groups with seemingly unrelated interests. The term 'strange bedfellows' is useful to describe the coalitions which may result from a common interest among disparate interest groups. A good example comes from the southern states of the US, a region often characterised by strong convictions and laws limiting the sale of alcoholic beverages to specific hours and days of the week (not Sundays). The Baptists, a religious group, sought restrictions on behaviour which they considered immoral. A law establishing state regulation of alcohol supports the Baptists' view that people are doing something wrong when they drink alcohol. Legislators who champion the anti-alcohol sentiment can count on the support of such groups when it comes to election time. The Baptists benefit from having less competition for the limited resources of their congregation, both of time and money. Such regulations also obviously serve the interests of government through tax collection from the government-owned monopoly of alcoholic beverage sales. Bootleggers (or smugglers) operate during the times when regulated facilities are closed and charge higher prices to cover the additional costs involved in evading the law. Smugglers who legally purchase cigarettes in low-tax states to be sold illegally in high-tax states have a similar interest in keeping high taxes on the books.

The 'strange bedfellows' analogy helps to explain how diverse special interests form coalitions. The concept applies to many seemingly unrelated environmental and natural resource issues. Despite their different goals, groups may agree on the need for control. They find themselves pushing for the same legislation, although they do not associate with one another or want to be perceived as such. Yet, given their similar legislative interests, they may be considered to act as a coalition, even though they may not actively collude. In this sense, any action which satisfies the disparate groups creates a coalition-type interest.

High-sulphur coal is an example of a product being made illegal through regulation. In the 1970s a coalition of environmentalists and high-sulphur coal producers sought removal of 97 per cent of the sulphur from all coal regardless of sulphur content.[1] Thus one can envisage such a coalition which shared an interest in requiring full scrubbing of high-sulphur coal even though cleaner air would be obtained from burning unscrubbed low-sulphur coal.

Command-and-Control versus Simple Rules

There are more obvious instances of coalitions which seek a government outcome from which they benefit but for which others pay. The administrative law bar and trial lawyers in the US have

---

[1] B. Ackerman and W. Hassler, *Clean Coal, Dirty Air: Or How the Clean Air Became a Multibillion-Dollar Bailout for High-Sulfur Coal Producers and What Should Be Done About It.* New Haven: Yale University Press, 1981; B. Yandle, 'Bootleggers, Baptists, and Political Limits', in B. Yandle, ed. *The Political Limits of Environmental Regulation*, Westport, CT: Quorum Books, 1989.

much to gain from regulations which subject individuals and firms to complex legal procedures. Fighting the Internal Revenue Service, securing an FCC licence, or challenging a Clean Air Act fine or regulation may be prohibitively expensive and therefore the more onerous regulations are unlikely to be contested. Professor Richard Epstein of the University of Chicago Law School argues that the 'command-and-control' approach which prescribes control technology to capture pollutants (for example, by catalytic converters and electrostatic precipitators) in the Clean Air Act, Federal Water Pollution Control Act, and other environmental quality laws fails to improve the environment, often favours one industry over another, and on occasion leads to endless lawsuits over how the government makes decisions.[2] He argues for the simple rule of the 'polluter pays'. Like F. A. Hayek,[3] Epstein argues that the traditional common law approach is more effective than complex regulation that imposes extensive information requirements on bureaucrats and lawmakers as they formulate, implement, and enforce laws. As a consequence of the information-processing requirements, the command-and-control system produces perverse incentives, inefficiency, and is unnecessarily costly.

Nevertheless, in Washington and Brussels there is a fast-growing army of business lobbyists and lawyers working for tougher and more complex environmental regulation. While some believe stringent regulations can produce social benefits, others (lawyers and lobbyists) see them as avenues for rent seeking by representing interest groups and people harmed by regulation (see Part I, Chapter 4: 'The Cost of Rent Seeking'). Environmental groups receive publicity attendant upon their participation in the regulatory process and thus raise funds from the general public. There are a number of ways such groups gain. Firms, on the other hand, have

---

[2] R. Epstein, *Simple Rules for a Complex World*, Cambridge, Mass.: Harvard University Press, 1995. See also, J. H. Fund, 'Common-Law Common Sense', *The Wall Street Journal*, 30 May 1995, p. A12.

[3] F. A. Hayek, *Law, Legislation, and Liberty*, 3 vols., London: Routledge & Kegan Paul; Chicago: University of Chicago Press, 1973–79.

learned that profits may be reaped by creating new markets or by protecting old ones against competitors.[4] 'Green' politicians have learned that being 'pro-green' does not ensure election but it may provide a political edge as they push legislation which appears to penalise business and protect endangered species and regional interests.

Bureaucrats, on the other hand, sleep well at night with the assurance that the 'environment' is an issue with sufficient public support for them to retain their jobs, emoluments of office and their pension rights. Further, they recognise that complex and often ineffective regulations serve their self-interest by justifying ever larger staff and budgets.

The Policy Debate

Public choice provides useful insights about how institutions affect public sector outcomes and how changing those institutions can make economic and environmental sense. Let us examine the Environmental Protection Agency's (EPA's) revision of the two standards for ozone and particulate matter (PM), also known as soot.

The pollution produced by one automobile causes trivial damage to the environment, whereas the cost to the owner of reducing this pollution can be considerable. On the other hand, the damage (externality) inflicted on the environment as a whole by automobile exhausts exceeds the aggregate cost to automobile owners of controlling emissions. From the standpoint of the neo classical economist, this is the basic argument for government intervention.[5] Given that the roads are government-owned and there is no road-pricing, the individual driver does not take into account his impact on other road users. Under these circumstances the government sets air quality standards so that human health and other important

---

[4] J. M. Buchanan and G. Tullock, 'Polluter's Profit and Political Response: Direct Controls Versus Taxes', *American Economic Review*, Vol. 66, No. 5, December 1976, pp. 983–84.

[5] For the contrasts between neo classical economics and public choice, see, for example, J. Wiseman, 'Principles of Political Economy: An Outline Proposal, Illustrated by Application to Fiscal Federalism', *Constitutional Political Economy*, Vol. 1, No. 1, Winter 1990, pp. 101–24.

objectives (plant and animal life, visibility, recreation, and scenic vistas) are protected. For an economist, the essence of setting an environmental standard for any pollutant, whether in air or water, consists in knowing whether tightening will produce additional benefits that exceed the additional costs. Since a zero emission standard is infinitely costly, it is necessary to undertake a cost-benefit analysis that answers the question: How clean is clean? In principle, this is a scientific question, but it cannot be extricated from political considerations. Public choice explains how the various forces interact (win or lose) in the context of political decision-making.

It has been assumed that if the law entails sufficiently stringent penalties, the dischargers of pollutants will simply do as they are told ('command and control') and also seek the least cost. But disincentives to compliance may be spawned by excessively burdensome regulations and hamper the achievement of regulatory targets. Stringent tax laws may spawn tax avoidance and evasion (see Part I, Chapter 6: 'Tax Avoision'). To the extent that highly burdensome rules are enforced, however, efficiency losses caused by excessive regulatory burdens may lower incomes and general living standards.

An example of harmful and unintended consequences is that making discharge limitations for new facilities much more stringent (called New Source Performance Standards) than those for existing facilities keeps old, heavy (and technologically less efficient) polluters such as electric power plants in operation longer.[6, 7]

Although the Clean Air Act (enacted in 1978) required the EPA to protect public health 'with an adequate margin' of safety and to

---

[6] See A. F. Abbot, G. L. Brady and M. T. Maloney, 'Political Limits of the Market for BAT Medallions', *Regulation*, Winter 1990; and G. L. Brady and M. T. Maloney, 'Capital Turnover and Marketable Pollution Rights', *Journal of Law & Economics*, 1988.

[7] Another example of an excessively stringent regulatory régime that exacerbates problems it was meant to solve is a ban on elephant hunting, coupled with limitations on the ivory trade, which drives up the price of ivory and encourages poaching, threatening elephant herds. This problem does not arise if elephant hunting is allowed when private property rights in elephants are established, thereby encouraging conservation by property owners who have an incentive to maintain elephant herds. (I. Sugg and U. Kreuter, *Elephants and Ivory: Lessons from the Trade Ban*, IEA Studies on the Environment No. 2, London: Institute of Economic Affairs, 1994.)

estimate benefits and costs, the Agency retorted that Congress required them to consider only the damages avoided and not the costs of prevention. So what explains their action? Public choice analysis requiring the EPA to estimate benefits and costs but not making it accountable for decisions taken is another example of institutional failure. Why did Congress stop short of establishing a cost-benefit decision rule? Public choice would imply that it is in the interest of the congressional oversight committee to make the EPA responsive to political pressures and thus make policy on the basis of political considerations, rather than the economic benefits and costs of proposals.

Cost-Benefit Analysis Applied to Particulate Matter and Ozone Standards

Although there are some sceptics, cost-benefit analysis can be an important tool in contemporary economics for evaluating the effectiveness of regulatory measures. In this case benefits are defined as the damages avoided from attaining a prescribed concentration of ozone. They include damage prevented to human health, scenic values, and ecosystem productivity. Costs include those incurred by meeting the prescribed concentrations and which are ultimately borne by consumers in the long run. These costs also include the impact of the price increases of the products on local and regional economic activities.

Public choice analysis can clarify our understanding of this issue. Given the expense of contesting the regulations there is a bias against accurately reflecting the cost borne by private individuals or firms which results in a bias towards the regulators' preferences. Furthermore, if the regulators' bias were towards fostering industrial activity, the outcome would be skewed in favour of a different set of political interests. We do not have to accept the validity of cost-benefit analysis to see how the decisions are necessarily biased one way or the other. Either way, it raises scepticism about the value of the exercise, for regulators use the taxpayers' resources to push interpretations which are in the regulators' interests.

Rent Seeking in Complex Regulation

A further public choice insight is obtained by viewing the Clean Air Act as a rent-seekers' paradise. The US regulatory framework has become a mechanism for restricting interregional competition by the enforcement of uniform national emission standards which discourage the movement of firms from the industrial North-east, the 'rust belt'. Still further arguments concern controlling growth, especially the activities of major corporations. Environmentalists see regulation as a system to punish the electric utilities and other larger sources of pollutants. Moreover, through the Clean Air Act and other environmental legislation of the 1970s, environmentalists succeeded in establishing the legal right to participate as injured parties regardless of the actual harm they may have experienced. This development has abrogated private property rights and has led to court decisions and regulations based on ideology or symbolism rather than actual damages incurred. Often the decisions were based on damages which were largely symbolic and then applied to situations in which the damages were speculative and difficult to quantify.

Existing firms see the Act as a means of cartelisation which discourages new competition. At the time the Clean Air Act was passed, firms did not resist the principal changes in their responsibilities under the law. They mistakenly thought that the emissions standards, the part of the Act that applied directly to them, could be addressed when enforcement reached the courts. However, some firms, especially the large polluters with many sources of emissions, pursued rent seeking through the complex regulatory system and managed to get a better deal from regulators than new dischargers subject to the relatively more stringent New Source Performance Standards (NSPS).

The Clean Air Act established regulations which set emission standards beyond those currently available. The object was to provide 'leverage' in defining 'acceptable' behaviour by dischargers. Congress mandated that the EPA fully embrace command-and-control's technology-forcing element as a means to impose immediate and readily enforceable federal controls on a relatively few widespread pollutants. 'Best Available Technology' (BAT) became what was 'currently available'. The effect, however, was to freeze pollution-control technology and discourage innovation. This occurred for two reasons. *First*, BAT procedures at the EPA monopolise the determination of control technology at the federal level despite differences in individual plants within firms and the environmental condition of the region in which they operate. *Second*, BAT requirements apply uniformly to all dischargers in a particular category. As such they waste many billions of dollars annually by ignoring variations in the cost of reducing pollution among individual plants within the same firm and among firms and industries, and by ignoring geographical variations in pollution effects.

BAT strategy imposes more stringent controls on new sources because there is no risk of a shutdown since the 'best available' exists only in the abstract. In order to win approval, new plants and products must endure lengthy regulatory proceedings, so the resulting uncertainty and delay discourage new investment and innovation by existing firms and provoke costly litigation. BAT also provides a continuing role for environmentalists and judges in this regulatory process. The 'all-or-nothing' regulation of pollutants has adverse effects: if firms were not required to use specific pieces of equipment, they might find more effective means of control which would reduce non-regulated but potentially dangerous pollutants.

Public choice illustrates the fact that when extensive regulation of a few pollutants is chosen, agency regulators stand to be big winners or losers and consequently have the incentive to distort information and stringently to enforce the rules.

Moreover, the command-and-control procedures provide fertile ground for litigation in the form of adversarial rule-making proceedings and protracted judicial review. It is often less costly for industries to invest in litigation than to comply with environmental regulations.

In summary, the BAT procedures provide the setting for rent seeking through the creation of complex regulations which require interpretation. The courts imposed on the EPA a very difficult role which it neither anticipated nor was equipped to handle. EPA regulators erroneously expected that the courts would require the states to enforce EPA mandates to achieve the goals of the Act. In many cases the Agency became both the producer and enforcer of plans at the state level when states could not or would not produce acceptable plans. That role required Congress to increase the Agency's budget by the amounts necessary to enforce state air quality programmes directly. In view of the size of the programme, Congress chose not to provide the necessary funding and the Act remains excessively stringent in uniform technology requirements at the national level but inadequately enforced at the level of the individual plant.

Summary and Conclusion

In its early years, the EPA sought to maximise a set of 'public interest goals', such as stringent outdoor air quality standards, stringent new source discharge standards, and stiff penalties for a few large polluters. Exogenous shocks – such as energy price increases, environmental risk information, new methodologies for estimating costs and benefits, and court decisions – changed the constraints facing EPA decision-makers and led to new regulatory programmes ('prevention of significant deterioration' and the height of smoke-stacks) to replace the old ones. In addition, the states refused to play the game by submitting plans to meet the EPA's goals. Also, the increase in energy prices brought on pressures for relaxation of environmental standards. Finally, there were a number of court decisions that placed the Agency at a bargaining disadvantage with the states. These caused the EPA to increase the degree of regulation and thus the opportunities for rent seeking. As information about costs was assimilated and both firms (stressing perceived costs) and special interest advocacy groups (stressing perceived benefits) were heard, the constraints facing the EPA changed so it engaged in efforts to expand its budget.

The failure of the US Clean Air Act teaches the public choice lesson that regulators or politicians need not face all the consequences of their decisions. A regulator will take all these into account only if the political process requires him do so. The failure to do so reflects the unwillingness of politicians to consider such issues. The Environmental Protection Agency will continue to shift the costs onto private property owners as long as the regulatory framework allows it to do so.

PART III

PUBLIC CHOICE

IN BRITAIN

Arthur Seldon

1

PUBLIC CHOICE OR

POLITICAL SOVEREIGNTY?

The Insights of Public Choice

PUBLIC CHOICE HAS DEVELOPED MANY INSIGHTS into the economic motives of politicians and the economic consequences of their political powers – by laws, rules and regulations, taxes and charges – to direct or influence individual lives.

Professor Tullock explains that 'people are people', subject to the same motivations in (so-called) 'public' life as in their private lives. This economic view of human motivation contrasts with the flawed view of political science which presents human beings as behaving very differently. They are then seen by many political scientists and sociologists as acting selflessly in 'public' life and selfishly in private ('commercial') life.

The analysis of 'public' choice has revealed that this distinction is a fallacy that has led to far-reaching error in the study and conduct of 'public life' in government. Even more, it has revealed the damaging effects on human liberties of the *over*-government generated by the system of 'democracy' in which the people have allowed themselves to be ruled by the representatives they elect hopefully to safeguard their interests.

Economists' deepening examination of 'public choice' in collective decision-making by government has revealed fundamental contrasts with decision-making by people in buying and selling as individuals, families, voluntary/spontaneous groups, firms or other units, in the day-to-day exchanges of markets.

The difference between the two systems of decision-making is fundamental and far-reaching. People exercise their decision-making in the political process as voters, in the market process as consumers.

Public choice is the relatively new study of the second-hand collective preferences or opinions of the people as voters in the political process in contrast to their first-hand individual preferences and choices as consumers in market exchange.

The questions that the political process does not answer are: How far should voter preferences outweigh consumer preferences, and in which goods and services? The economic process of exchange solves the question of how far consumer preferences shall prevail.

Collective and Individual Decision-Making

By the end of the three Parts of this Readings it will become apparent to newcomers to the subject that the distinction between collective and individual decision-making is the often ignored key to the very different consequences for living standards, personal liberties in all aspects of life, and the prospects of amity in national and international relations.

It will also have emerged in all three Parts that the term 'public choice' is a misleading name for a system of economics and politics in which the choices of the real public are not generally satisfied by the political 'public' institution of collective decision-making. The ultimate truth is that the politicised 'public' institutions are not primarily concerned with the choices of the real public as individuals or families.

The essential reason is that collective decisions are made by representatives of the public, not by the public themselves. The indirect results that emerge in the politically-decided production of goods and services are usually very different from those that would be chosen directly by the public itself.

* * * * * *

The working of 'public choice' in principle is presented by Professor Tullock in Part I and illustrated in Parts II and III from its working in real life in Anglo-American countries. Dr Brady illustrates public choice in Part II from government policy on the conduct and rules governing industry in the United States. Part III examines the working of public choice mainly in British 'social welfare' and allied services. The analysis helps to explain why collective choice displaced individual choice for over a century in much of industry in the USA and in most of 'welfare' in the UK. It thus also shows why, in both countries but especially in the UK where collective choice has advanced further than in the USA, government has finally outlasted its utility in much or most of both industry and welfare, and why it will be increasingly replaced in the 21st century in both countries as incomes rise and technological advance supplies services more suited to individual preferences.

The British welfare services discussed are mainly education, medical care, housing for people with low incomes, insurance against interruptions of earnings in sickness, unemployment and retirement, and protection against everyday risks.

Government and Public Goods

The increasing displacement of collective by individual decision has changed the focus of interest in democracy and revealed the continuing *over*-government it has generated. So far, from the end of the 18th to virtually the early 21st century, the political debate between leading economists has centred essentially on the necessary or desirable functions of government. These were generally thought to be the 'public goods' that it was supposed only government could supply. The focus has now to change from the necessary or desirable functions of government to the *incapacity* of government to limit itself to the necessary or desirable public goods. The central debate in politics and economics is moving from what government 'should' do to what it *can* do when people find better services outside the state. And the long-apparent necessity to move large tracts of earnings from individuals to government by taxation or other means is being increasingly questioned.

The fundamental distinction is now increasingly between which services government *should* provide, which has been the long-lived concern of political science, and those it *can* provide when there is rapid advance in economic life and government functions can be replaced by superior services in markets. What government can do is increasingly decided by changes in the two fundamental components of economic life – supply and demand – which the political process often ignores at severe cost to the people. What government should do – how large or small it should be – was long debated by the opposing schools of economic thought which argued that it should do as little as necessary or as much as possible.

The English economist J.M. Keynes clarified an essential difference in the thinking on the functions of government – that it should do only what the people could not do at all, not what it could do better than the people. The caution was timely when he wrote in 1932 (in *The End of Laissez Faire*[1]) but it has been largely ignored in the last 60 years by politicians in their anxiety to achieve or maintain power. What government began to do in social welfare and elsewhere in the last decades of the 19th century it was rarely ready to abandon even when, in the 20th century, individuals showed they could do both more for themselves and better than could be provided by government.

The New Distinction – What Government Will Be Able to Do

The new distinction in the functions of government in the 21st century – what it will be able to do – is even more fundamental because it weakens or removes from government the power to continue with many services it has long thought to be its essential functions. So far government has persisted in supplying – and extending – supposedly essential services begun in the 19th and 20th centuries. They were standardised for all, or increasingly most, of the people and ranged from the mediocre in quality to the blatant denial of personal choice. For the mass of the people with lower incomes there seemed no alternative. Increasingly since the 1950s, even as incomes rose and technological invention accelerated, standardised state services were continued when more people could obtain services that better suited individual and family preferences.

---

[1] J. M. Keynes, The End of Laissez Faire, *Keynes: Collected Writings*, (ed.) D. Moggridge, Vol. IX, 272–94, Macmillan, 1972, was heralded by the politically minded as a far-seeing tract for the future. Since the 1939–45 World War it has been increasingly rendered out of date by technological invention that has raised incomes and enabled people as consumers to replace government as producers. The much-neglected evidence has been analysed in Arthur Seldon, *The Dilemma of Democracy: The Political Economics of Over-Government*, Hobart Paper No. 136, London: Institute of Economic Affairs, 1998.

The standardised state services became increasingly inadequate. Yet until recently there seemed to be no escape for the millions of people with the lowest incomes. In the new century the increasing power to buy better than the state can supply, and the general dissatisfaction with the standardised state, will accelerate.

Reluctance to Pay for State Services

Moreover, there has been increased parallel reluctance to pay for state services indirectly by taxes or directly by charges. In Britain the illusion that the state has the infinite resources and the supposed moral duty to supply 'public services' whatever their quality, their denial of individual liberty, and their costs, long fostered by politicians and sociologists, has paralysed public discussion and scholarly thought. In recent years other methods of payment for services exchanged privately between individuals and groups have, moreover, appeared on a growing scale in the form of barter and in the replacement of office or factory by home working (a 20th-century advanced form of the 'domestic system' of the 18th century) based on the new range of computers, word processors and the latest telecommunication devices. This shift in the work-place is accompanied on much larger scales by electronic money and Internet transactions between strangers in unknown countries and continents.

The distinction between tax avoidance and evasion in the methods of paying for government goods or services, whether sanctioned or disallowed by the law, became blurred. Increasingly, in the last 15 years, the state has begun to lose the power to raise the funds required for its stubbornly continued personal welfare services, especially education, medical care and housing, all of which have failed to keep pace with the rising quality and standards of food, clothing, domestic comforts and personal amenities bought increasingly in open markets by people with lower but rising incomes.

The latest phase in the retreat of government is for state schools to ask parents for voluntary donations or gifts of equipment. The state hospitals have long looked to patients' families and friends to provide secondary 'non-medical' comforts and facilities. Government housing is increasingly outdated by new homes that the state cannot match. And government in Britain can no longer assemble the funds required to fulfil its undertaking to supply acceptable income in the predictable or unpredictable vicissitudes of life – sickness, unemployment and ageing.

The Failure of State Welfare Services

The general trend is that democratic government in Britain is failing to maintain the range and flexibility of its welfare services in comparison – and therefore competition – with supplies available in the newest shops and stores in town and country. The increasingly everyday evidence of outdated government supplies and services, and therefore in the very rôle of government, raises the crucial issue for the politics of democracy: When will representative government have to accept that it is not competent to cope with the opportunities and expectations of the future?

Insofar as there are industrial, political and cultural similarities between the United Kingdom and the United States the observations on each country in Parts II and III apply to the other. And, insofar as such differences persist, the vital task of the real 'public's choice' is to ensure that government reflects private preferences. The people of Britain have yet to emulate the power of Americans to create the political mechanisms that reflect their individual preferences. On both the supply and demand sides of economic life the American economy is far advanced over the British. Personal incomes in the USA are about 2.25 times those of the UK, and the economy is much more competitive and productive because producers in all states know they can specialise within the federal market of 275 million consumers rather than the UK market of 59 million. The political power of federal and state governments in the USA to deny private preferences did not advance as far as that of the increasingly socialising policies of the British central governments of all parties – Conservative, Liberal and Labour – over the last century. And the much larger markets of American industry over the 50 states have enabled Americans to escape from over-government into private exchange more readily than in Britain.

Voting Systems and Voters' Preferences

The fundamental elements of public choice analysed in Part I – the fraudulent voting system that frustrates rather than faithfully reflecting voter preferences, the pursuit of rent seeking, the rewards of logrolling, the self-interested bureaucracy, the chronically excessive taxation, and the failure to confine legislation to its irreducible 'federal' economic limits – will be seen at work in the large parts of the British economy in which government persistently provides services which are clearly personal and family, though misleadingly described as 'public' or 'social'.

These characteristic features of representative democracy have had fundamental but often undesirable effects on the British welfare services. The precarious voting systems of 'democracy' revealed by Professor Tullock, and demonstrated in Part II and below, do not, or cannot, faithfully reflect the preferences of voters. A passing temper of impatience among voters with a government, as in Britain with both political parties in 1979 and 1997, can produce a large change to its opposite rival for many years, much longer than the days or weeks required to change between shops. Undeclared logrolling between representatives in the British Parliament who know little of one another's special interests, which they may even think harmful, enables them to serve their personal political interests at the expense of unsuspecting voters. Rent seeking by British voters organised predominantly as producers – in recent years typically miners, teachers, railway workers, state health or local government employees mobilised in national trade unions – has extracted undeserved privileges at the long-term expense of unorganised consumers. The ignored irony in this producer pressure on government is that the victims are often themselves as consumers.

The Power of the Bureaucracy

Not least, strategically placed bureaucrats, better-informed than their political masters, advise the adoption of policies that fundamentally serve their bureaucratic interests or reinforce their prospects by organising voting pressure. In view of the large numbers of government staffs – from administrative and electronic through medical and pedagogic to clerical and manual organised in

141

professional associations and trade unions – the question raised by Professor Tullock, whether 'public officials' should sacrifice the right to vote as an improper influence on their employment interests, will before long have to be faced in Britain.

Populist causes – disguised as the sanctity of 'public services' – are used by government to justify taxes otherwise rejected or resented by tax-payers. Government has been inflated beyond its optimum limits. It should be decentralised and confined to its irreducible boundaries.

2

GOVERNMENT INTENTIONS

AND CONSEQUENCES

The Economics of Politics

'PUBLIC CHOICE' IS THE ACADEMIC NAME for the analysis of the powers and decisions of government made for the supposed good of the people. A better description is 'the economics of politics', for three reasons. The *first* and most obvious is that analysed by Professor Tullock in his Chapter 1: with rare historical exceptions, political power does not transform people into selfless saints or all-wise seers. The *second* is the less obvious reason, still generally overlooked or denied by political scientists and sociologists, that elected government (or any other collection of individuals) cannot judge the individual preferences of the people it is designed to represent. And the *third* is the historic evidence that, even where the collectives begin by putting the people first, they end in putting the people second and themselves first by continuing their activities long after economic change has made them undesirable, superfluous and resented.

A crucial purpose of public choice economics is to analyse the motives of individuals in government – as politicians, their advisers, 'public servants', senior bureaucrats and their aides. It identifies their objects and functions as men and women in 'public' life and reveals whether, if at all and how, they differ in contrast with the objects of individuals in 'private' life.

Public and Private Purposes

Professor Tullock concludes from his analysis of public choice that human motives are fundamentally the same in public as in private lives. The supposed contrast between public and private purposes is largely fictional. People in private activities, who work in competitive markets, have to do real public good because if they fail they can be more easily and sooner deserted by escape to competing suppliers. There is no such ready escape from political government. People in public life claim to act selflessly in the interests of 'the people'; but in practice they put their personal interests first.

The word 'public' is among the most abused terms in the English language, certainly in politics. The study of public choice reveals its misuse. The London School of Economics economist, Frederick Hayek, who built the powerful 1930s fusion of classical English/Scottish and Austrian liberal thinking, wrote in his last book, *The Fatal Conceit*,[1] of the confusion produced by the frequently-used but question-begging term 'social'. It was often carelessly employed to imply selfless activity for the benevolent 'general good' in contrast with the private individual activity that is supposedly designed for selfish personal, 'commercial', advantage.

In Britain, much the same distinction has been conveyed by social scientists in their simplistic contrasts of 'public' with 'private'. The insinuation is that 'public' means selfless or benevolent whereas 'private' means selfish or greedy. Hence the emphasis on the benevolent and desirable 'public interest', 'public service', 'public expenditure', 'public investment', 'public enterprise', and a range of services from 'public transport' to 'public libraries'. It is the most misleading word in the vocabulary of politics, where it is even more question-begging than 'fair', 'reasonable', 'appropriate' or 'just'. The politician who wants to sell a doubtful policy he cannot explain or justify calls it 'in the public interest' – or by the nebulous 'fair'.

Moreover, 'public' blessings are contrasted with the opposite self-interested and therefore undesirable 'private interest', 'private service', 'private expenditure', 'private investment', 'private enterprise', 'private transport', 'private libraries', and many more.

The implication is that objectionable 'private' activities are in principle – when chosen, produced, and distributed by supposedly

---

[1] F. A. Hayek, *The Fatal Conceit: The Errors of Socialism*, London: Routledge, 1988, and Chicago: University of Chicago Press, 1989.

disinterested representatives of the people in legislative assemblies – superior to the goods or services chosen and preferred by the people themselves and obtained by voluntary private exchange and trade.

The distinction is patently false. Yet its falsehood has been suppressed by the persistent teaching since the 18th century of the precarious proposition that representative political assemblies know more about the condition of the people who elect them – their wants, 'needs', preferences – than the people know themselves.

A Fictional Distinction

The verdict of history in Britain – in the final consequences of the welfare state and its 'social' welfare – does not support the fictional distinction between 'public' and 'private'. It may be convenient to allow representatives in Parliament to organise some services for a time – perhaps years, some as long as decades – until individuals can supply them better for themselves and one another. In Britain there were some such necessary or desirable 'public goods' – from defence to 'public health' precautions of the growing industrial towns – even in the period of *laissez-faire* free trade in the mid-19th century. But the historical evidence shows that once the representatives exercise government control of 'public' services they do not vary them with the ability and desire of the people before long to supply them for themselves. 'Public goods' tend to become permanent even when people can arrange them better privately.

In Britain what should have been a few years of political control were stretched into centuries. There is no formal British parallel for the American 'sunset' industries or public services that are ended when they become superfluous. In Britain, it seems, once a 'public' service always a 'public' service. At the turn of the 19th to the 20th century no less than half of them could in time have been transferred to free exchange between individuals and firms – the remaining so-called 'basic industries' like fuel and transport, certainly most of education and medical care, all 'Council' (local government) housing, most pension saving, insurance against interruption of earnings by industrial adaptation to changing technology, and most of local government services. Many are still kept as 'public services' by the political influence of the rent-seeking trade unions and professional organisations.

Politicians and the 'Public Interest'

The claim of British politicians to serve the public interest is, with few exceptions, baseless. The theory of the superiority of public over private services is both a myth and an internal contradiction. It is a myth because in the real world it is not safe to allow political representatives to exercise outdated powers to provide 'public' services. British history reveals that in the long run the people would have been better advised to discover new private ways to produce and distribute goods and services that are used jointly than to run the risks of almost permanent, inefficient, wasteful control by political representatives. If they are better produced jointly, people long ago would have found new ways to produce them jointly in voluntary, flexible organisations without the use of political representatives.

The Myth of Collective Superiority

There is a conceivable condition in which individuals cannot or will not move to produce a service unless all agree and all pay. The obvious case is defence against external danger. But that is hardly likely in personal services such as education, medical care, homes or insuring against interruptions in income like unemployment. These 'welfare' services satisfy intensely personal requirements that vary widely with individual circumstances or preferences. And all can be bought from suppliers who provide services to suit individual requirements. Moreover, as incomes rise, and state services such as education and medical care in Britain today deteriorate, more families will pay for them by school fees and health insurance. The myth of collective superiority is being gradually destroyed by changing supply and demand in open markets. The claim that welfare is a 'public good' is being abandoned.

The notion that political representatives can serve the people better when people become more capable of dispensing with them as their incomes rise is even more implausible. In the course of economic development, such as that since the late 18th century, incomes of all the people – from the richest to the poorest – have risen unexpectedly fast. The rise was not uniform down the years or similar in all income groups, but the general movement has made the children of one generation much wealthier than their parents and especially their grandparents. As life-expectancy has grown with improving health by the conquest of disease, especially in recent decades, the 25-year generations have grown to 30 years. The children have become twice to three times as rich as their parents. Few 'working-class' British people would now choose to live in a government-built Council house. They would much prefer a refund of taxes or a housing voucher with which to choose a home, a health voucher with which to avoid long queues for doctors, medicines and hospitals, an education voucher to escape from the worst state schools, as they now use luncheon or travel vouchers from their employers to choose meals or means of transport.

Returning 'Welfare' to the Private Sector

The obvious conclusion is that, as national income rises, the state can return its few unavoidable 'social' welfare activities to private welfare suppliers. That could have been the history of British life since the last war. Political power has fanned the naïve notion that, as national income rises, the state should demand more of it to spend on public services. It seems to have escaped social historians that national income has increased because personal earnings have been raised, mostly by individual effort and enterprises, making much state activity superfluous. The state could be reducing the taxes it raises for outdated activities, leaving the citizen with the added advantages of widening choices in satisfying personal requirements.

3

OVER-DEPENDENCE ON

THE WELFARE STATE

IT IS A SEVERE REFLECTION ON UNIVERSITY TEACHING OF THE SOCIAL SCIENCES in Britain that the lesson for policy-makers and their servants was lost in the political theology of the welfare state. That rising family incomes could reduce the writ of the state, and with it the power of politicians and their servants over private family life, has rarely been discussed, or even contemplated, by enthusiasts for the welfare state.

In spite of the broad historic progression in incomes and living conditions the opposite notion, common among well-meaning supporters of the early social services, was that they should be extended on the apparently obvious ground that, as incomes rose, the tax revenue of government would also rise. This apparently generous impulse has been revealed as a simplistic *non sequitur*.

The LSE and Enlargement of the Welfare State

At the leading centre of British university scholarship in the social sciences in the inter-war years, the London School of Economics (LSE), the thinking of the Founders (Beatrice and Sidney Webb) and their ardent Fabian followers encouraged the view that higher private and therefore national incomes should enlarge the functions of the state. The *non sequitur* escaped the Fabians and their successors. This simplistic teaching was rejected by the liberal school of economists at the LSE nurtured by Edwin Cannan and later led by Austrian-born Frederick Hayek and the British Lionel Robbins, with their gifted younger teaching colleagues, not least J.R. Hicks and R.H. Coase, both, with Hayek, eventually Nobel Laureates. Yet the *non sequitur* has lingered in the teaching of social sciences in British universities generally where it has spread from the LSE.

The truth is precisely the opposite. For several post-war decades after 1946 the welfare *non sequitur* persisted at the London School of Economics with re-emphasis under the sociologist Richard Titmuss. More recently it has been revived under another sociologist, the new London School of Economics Director from Cambridge, Anthony Giddens, who claims to have discovered a nebulous 'third way' between political and private choice, the state and the market, which the economist scholars who built the 1930s LSE would have scorned as losing both – the fading advantages of the state and the growing advantages of individual choice.

Rejecting the Fabian Fiction

By chance a foremost independent thinker of the Webbian–Fabian tradition declared its tragic errors in early 1999. A Church of England journal published his historic rejection of the Fabian fiction as Part III of this *Primer* was being completed.[1] He has now emerged as the rare social scientist, with personal experience of developing a benevolent lobby for children, elected to the status of a government Minister in 1998, which he abandoned when he found his revisionist thinking did not suit the philosophy or short-term intentions of the 1997 government. He described his challenging magisterial theme on the welfare state as 'What, Then, was Unthinkable?'. His testament, a reasoned rebuke to his political friends, vividly illustrates the working of public choice in practice.

In Part I, Chapter 3, on 'Logrolling', Professor Tullock recounts his surprise on discovering on a visit to England in the 1970s that British parliamentarians, including a former Cabinet Minister, were apparently not aware of logrolling in day-to-day Parliamentary practice. He learned from a Member of Parliament that members of the House of Commons generally and habitually exchanged voting support for one another's attempts to introduce legislation in which

---

[1] Frank Field, MP, in 'What was Unthinkable?', *Crucible*, published by the Board for Social Responsibility, Church House, Westminster, London SW1P 3NZ, 1998. All the quotations in the discussion that follows are cited from the above source.

they were personally not involved nor even personally interested. This was logrolling in the Mother of Parliaments.

If, presumably, no money changed hands, British logrolling was the exchange of services by barter, which elsewhere facilitates the escape from taxes. But its importance was more general and questionable.

The lack of knowledge – or state of ignorance – by British voters of logrolling between Members of Parliament remains to this day. The exchange of voting might support or oppose Parliamentary permission to build roads or other large-scale structures that could be worth millions of pounds to pressure groups and their lobbies. They may be seen as innocent or possibly harmful, even, in the technical sense analysed by Professor Tullock, 'immoral'. They may be as innocent or as immoral as evidently practised on a large scale in the USA Congress 100-member upper house Senate and the 450-member lower House of Representatives.

The 'thinking-the-unthinkable' declaration is that of Frank Field, for several months Minister of Welfare Reform during 1998 in the 1997 New Labour Government. His long experience as a pioneer in formulating social policy for children in low-income families has led him, after his recent painfully short term of office and resignation, to formulate new thinking on the fundamentals of welfare policy. The central theme is how the welfare state will have to be changed fundamentally to reflect the latest developments in rising incomes, family life and attitudes to paying taxes.

Mr Field's clearly presented text reveals the historic change in his approach to the political practice of public choice – the collective supply of welfare by government – analysed in this Primer. His latest thinking elaborates the new policies – a combination of private and state arrangements for supplying income in unemployment, sickness and other conditions – that must now replace the mistaken Fabian-Titmuss philosophy of 'higher incomes therefore more social welfare'. And it raises the most fundamental dilemma in human existence, examined by economists analysing the future but not always by other social scientists overwhelmed by the past, that the prevailing universal scarcity of resources, finally recognised after decades of self-delusion, requires government to confess that more given to some people means less available for others.

'Titmuss believed', says Mr Field, 'that we were on the threshold of abundance…', the unknown condition in which there is plenty for all, so that more for some does not reduce what is available to others.

> '…In an age of abundance', Titmuss argued, 'the production of consumption goods will become a subsidiary question for the West… Welfare could be delivered by government to all citizens free of conditions and obligations. …universal welfare services could help establish a basic equality between individuals…'

This was the fatal Fabian fallacy in thinking on the welfare state. In setting this goal, said Field, Titmuss '…followed the political tradition of R.H. Tawney [the highly-respected Fabian socialist scholar] whose ideas about equality sprang from his view that …men and women were created equal'. But, continued Field, 'the age of abundance was still far off. *Welfare was still a scarce good.*' (My italics.) Given human nature, individuals were likely to respond more carefully if the benefits they were drawing had been earned and were not presented as a free good. The truth at last. Hallelujah!

'Altruism', Field warned, 'might be expressed within small groups such as families or very close friendships. But it was not a motive on which the institutions of wider society could be safely governed.' Frank Field has bravely declared the emptiness of a century of Fabian fable.

These 'institutions of wider society' are the collective services and institutions supplied 'free' – the state schools, universities, hospitals, homes and much else – built by government elected by representative democracy. They are the benevolent institutions long advocated as universally the task of government. But in the real world, as analysed by public choice, human nature is not more benevolent and may be less benevolent in public choice than in private lives. Electing men and women as representatives in government, or appointing men and women as 'public' officials, does not transform them into saints or seers. The thinking of representatives and officials, said Field:

'was that universal provision was possible only through a state-run scheme. [But] only by *separating* the need for universal provision from a state monopoly [will] it be possible to extend the universal ideal'.

Separating Universal Provision from State Monopoly

This is the separation that British politicians in all parties are now in the 21st century having to re-examine and confess in abject humility. But most still cannot wholly accept the abandonment of the welfare state because it implies confession of a century and more of political irresponsibility and intellectual error. The longer it is prolonged the more severe the error since 1946–48 when the welfare state was last expanded by the post-war governments.

'The reality running through much of this revisionism', continued Field relentlessly, in the modern dilemma of over-government 'under-funded' by a reluctant tax-paying people, 'was an attempt to come to terms with the public's attitude to the payment of taxes and the receipt of services.'

'There was', he added with the candour still unfamiliar among his former political colleagues, 'and there is a resistance to the payment of taxes, yet there continues to be a demand for high quality public services.' A most fundamental change had taken place in the electorate's views.

Why? 'A number of factors were at work … Rising living standards have increased the resistance to the tax-take on incomes.'

And here emerged the truth long concealed by the Fabian teaching at the London School of Economics: 'As real incomes have risen, so too have the choices open to individuals on how that income might be spent. And these are the choices that *individuals themselves increasingly want to make*.' (My italics.)

'Instead of merely railing against this change, thinking the unthinkable was about accepting it as the framework within which the development of welfare should take place.' Field added, to his old friends: 'The challenge … was how to make the promise of universal service compatible with this new set of voter preferences.'

But, as the analysis of public choice indicates, the next step would be politically delicate because it would reveal the unwelcome truth –

the underlying philosophic and political reluctance of recent British governments to lose their power to run the state.

'The aim', said Field, 'was to show how it was possible, with the restraint taxpayers now imposed on policy-makers, to achieve an adequate universal provision of pensions.' His solution was 'to form a partnership with the private and mutual ["not-for-profit" in the American term] sectors.'

This is the new blasphemy in British politics that the 1997 government, reluctantly and cautiously, is having to approach and embrace. But even more fundamental reform will have to be contemplated. The emerging task was 'how best to police welfare expenditure', that is, to ensure that the newly recognised scarce resources were spent with due regard for the economic theory of marginal returns to displaced alternatives: that to maximise the use of tax revenue the marginal utility (usefulness) in alternatives used would have to be equalised so that £100 million spent on 'free' schools would do at least as much good as £100 million withheld from 'free' medical care.

Tawney, Titmuss and Unlimited Resources

The fundamental Tawney-Titmuss fiction of unlimited resources has been, and still is, influential. The 1940–45 war-time all-party government led by Winston Churchill accepted the 1942 Report on Social Services prepared by Sir William Beveridge, the former Director of the London School of Economics, in the 1930s. He had also been in 1911 adviser to the then-Liberal Ministers, Lloyd George and Winston Churchill, on the first national insurance scheme, financed through the state by 'social insurance contributions' and taxes. Here, Field rightly says,

'what was surprising was that Beveridge [in 1942] seemed willing to ignore so many of the lessons he had learned over the previous 40 years ... like the Webbs and most of the reformers he was intrigued by the startling social advance by so many of the skilled working class during the late Victorian and Edwardian era' –

from the 1880s to 1910.

The vital truths staunchly faced by Frank Field, more than by any politicians or academics in the new 1997 government, recognised the improving conditions in working-class life as the source of the errors made by those who urged the expansion of the welfare state. Their guilty failure was to overlook the massive progress in working-class living standards and the associated mechanisms for voluntary working-class insurance that were produced, not by the politicians in the political process using the force of law but by private individuals in the market helping the people to help themselves.

The Failure of Social Historians...

It was the failure of the social historians to recognise the origins and extent of voluntary insurance that falsely validated the unnecessary – and flawed – state insurance system. It has finally damaged democracy, and is now intensifying the dilemma which arises because it has expanded too far and cannot withdraw for fear of losing its political supporters. But it is being increasingly escaped by the same people as consumers and taxpayers. 'The engine of such social advance,' records Field, 'was located ... in the friendly society movement.' These were the voluntary 'mutuals'. It was here in the early 20th century that the newly-formed Labour Party made the first of its many mistakes in defence of its then members in the working-classes.

Field withdrew in 1998 from the government formed by his political party because, as an independent-minded thinker, he put what he saw as the real world of human beings in families before the requirements of government anxious to maintain public popularity by avoiding disliked reforms.

It may now be clear why 'public choice' has been redefined in this section of the *Primer* as 'the economics of politics'. The new Secretary of State for Social Security, Mr Alastair Darling, saw public choice as 'the politics of economics'. Professor Tullock's outline of the principles of public choice in Part I suggests that government Ministers may justifiably see their task as, above all, to maintain their government and political party in office even if they put last the policies that would best serve the long-term interests of the people.

But the new Labour rebel against the Fabian fallacy now puts the long-term interests first. He speaks of 'downsizing the state'. This is the fundamental classical liberal view that as incomes rise the state can do less. It would have been political blasphemy in the previous Labour government when in power in 1974–79. Remarkably and courageously he now urges his political friends to accept that 'the only sure foundation for welfare [is] to build on ...the natural impulse in most of us to look after ourselves and those we most love' – by which he means essentially the family.

The historic testament by Field enforces reflection on the economics of government – of frustrated 'public choice' in its literal sense – that permitted the wide contrast between the changing personal and family circumstances of the people and the forms of government they had allowed to develop and tolerate over the past 150 years.

...and the Failings of Democracy

Field's final thought – that people must be allowed to put first those nearest to them – reveals the failure of democracy. The question remains what the new policies are to be. The new circumstances of the 21st century make them very different from those of the late 19th century. The working people of those years from the 1880s may have done their best with voluntary societies. Their increasingly middle-class children and grandchildren will now want to use all possible mechanisms for insurance against loss of income and will want the most efficient, whether private or state, 'for-profit' or 'not-for-profit'. That means they will want to use the techniques that make for fastest progress – the competitive market and its full range of the latest advances in communications and in methods of payment, not least those that minimise tax imposts.

That is the structure of representative government produced by political power that will resist change and has finally provoked the *'Dilemma of Democracy'*.[2] Democracy has now grown too far beyond the acceptable functions and services of the state that the people once

---

[2] A. Seldon, *The Dilemma of Democracy, op. cit.*

accepted because they could not provide better themselves by market production and exchange. But economic and technical advance create new 'escapes' from outdated government by tax rejections, informal domestic and business exchange/trading and other devices that are difficult for government to trace in the growing parallel economy, ignored by most social scientists.

Beveridge's Error

Beveridge's error was, surprisingly for a Liberal Member of Parliament, that he under-estimated the extent of the expansion in what Samuel Smiles would have called 'self-help'. The extent of pre-First World War voluntary working-class social insurance was much larger than Beveridge had revealed in his 1942 Report. In the 1972 IEA historical study, *The Long Debate on Poverty*, on the misleading writings of Charles Dickens and other 'state of England' novelists who distorted fact to write fiction, Dr Charles Hanson, the economic historian at Newcastle University, revealed the error was still being made in 1947.[3] I had gone to consult Beveridge, as a fellow-member of the Liberal Party, on technical details of state pensions. I found him writing *Voluntary Action*, his apologia or lament for the demotion of the voluntary societies from insurers to administrative agents of the 1949 state insurance. But he was still under-estimating their coverage. Dr Hanson found that, by omitting the unregistered friendly and other voluntary societies in 1947, Beveridge had failed to discover that only a small minority of working men had not yet insured against sickness and old age by 1909.

By the first year of the 21st century the error on voluntary insurance is now the opposite. To strengthen his case for extension of 'social' (state) insurance Beveridge, in 1942, says Mr Field rightly, had 'exaggerated … the inadequacy of voluntary insurance'. In the new century the new aspirations of the higher-income working people will urge them to seek out the most efficient and fastest mechanisms, whether 'public' or private. They will supplement the

---

[3] C. G. Hanson, 'Welfare Before the Welfare State', in A. Seldon (ed.), *The Long Debate on Poverty*, IEA Readings No. 9, London: Institute of Economic Affairs, 1972, pp. 111–39.

best of the 'not-for-profit' organisations by the newest with shareholders who will insist on the most efficient directors and mechanisms. The obstacle will remain that the economics of politics in democratic government, the process of 'public choice', will induce democracy to over-emphasise the risks of human life in the 21st century, as it had done in the 20th.

The evidence of British history is still foreign to the social historians and the sociologists. It is that the main services of what became 'the welfare state' suffered from three crucial defects in disregarding the changing conditions of the people:

- They were introduced *too soon* by false argument and before the private mechanisms could show their superiority.

- They were maintained *too large* in forms that did not respond to or reflect individual private wishes.

- And they were continued *far too long* when they had become superfluous because the people could provide them privately with better regard for individual preferences.

Experience demonstrates clearly that the 'public choice' delivered by government contrasts, sometimes moderately, often sharply, with the private choices of the people. Knowledge is discovered continuously down the centuries, sometimes slowly, often quickly. Knowledge has developed in free societies by teaching personal skills that encourage individuals to benefit and enrich each other, or often one another, by exchanging knowledge of skills and eventually goods and services. In time they learn to concentrate (specialise) on the skills they acquire most easily. They move on to pure barter without money, then learn to use portable or durable objects in common use as money. They eventually end by separate stages of buying and selling in places, at times and in markets that suit them best.

Transferring Social and Welfare Services to the Public Sector

Most of the goods and services now described in Britain as 'social' or 'welfare' began to be bought and sold by exchanges in markets from the early 1800s. In the past 200 years continuing advance in technology and sciences would have refined the scientific and exchange mechanisms. By now, and advancing rapidly in the 2000s, the British would have developed specialisation and private exchange between individuals, families, and small groups of the goods and services now falsely called 'social' or 'welfare'.

Unfortunately, excuses for transferring them from private people to 'public servants' were found. The private services – especially education, medical care and pensions – were condemned by social historians as growing too slowly: they were rejected as providing for only small numbers of people. Only government, they said, could accelerate their growth to cover most or all of the people.

From around the 1870s the political process of electing representatives in government to supply 'public choice' was developed by both the Conservative and Liberal parties. And once the goods and services were transferred from 'private' to 'public' they were expanded and made comprehensive and eventually became established and unquestioned parts of national life.

It is historic fiction to argue that these services could not be expanded to satisfy more of the people but had to be supplied – or supplied better – by the political process and elected government. The tragedy for private personal lives is that, once captured by the 'representative' collective organisations, with their falsifying voting, rent seeking, logrolling, and the rest of the paraphernalia of 'public choice', ordinary people were denied the methods of production and distribution, and buying and selling developed by private barter and exchange down the centuries.

For 130 years since about 1870 – since the Gladstone-Forster Education Act of that year – people have been seduced into accepting the fiction that if left to their lowly life-styles, low incomes, and passive acceptance of authority they would neglect their families and themselves. They would not pay school fees or insure for medical care; they would live in mean housing; they would risk poverty in old age.

So the 1870 Education Act introduced 'free' government schooling even though three in four working-class children had attended private fee-paid schools (paid by parents assisted by the church and charities) since 1860 and earlier. In 1911 the Social Insurance Act coerced into state insurance 12 million working-class male employees when nine million were covered by Friendly Society and other private insurers. In 1921 local authorities began building the council housing that deteriorated into the slums and later high-rise tower-blocks in which their tenants' children will not wish to live. And in 1949 the post-war state pensions were enlarged but in 1998 were found inadequate for an increasingly affluent populace.

The Harm Done by the Welfare State
The final irony is that the welfare state – ostensibly created to better the people in most need – has done most harm. The welfare policy that was being outdated by irrepressible long-term economic advance has been prolonged by short-term political patching-up of services that have been found wanting and are being rejected by the people as inadequate and outdated. In Britain recent governments have been spending large sums of taxpayers' money to patch the buildings – and retain the staffs – of schools, hospitals and institutions that are becoming outdated. And in the most recent government only one Minister, Mr Field, a close student of British society who became a politician, has spoken the inconvenient truths – and lasted only a few months in office. 'Public choice' in the political process has never represented the real choices of the real public.

4

THE WEAKENING OF THE FAMILY

A CONSEQUENCE THAT CLEARLY FOLLOWS FROM THE TENACITY OF THE WELFARE STATE is the weakening of the British family by the continuing displacement of parents by political agents.

Historians give it scant attention in their accounts of social policies. Sociologists have only lately confessed government errors in policy affecting the family – faulty money grants, mismanaged local authority homes for the neglected aged, the lonely single mothers, the abused children removed from families into 'public' institutions in which they were supposed to be safe, and mismanaged local authority homes for neglected grandparents.

Separating Children from Parents

Yet few, if any, historians or sociologists trace the effects of the over-long century of state welfare services that separated the natural links of dependence and affection between parents and children. Through peace and war, boom and slump, summer and winter, decade after decade, the mass of British children has been accustomed to accept that their parents have little competence and virtually no influence on their schooling, their medical care by doctors and nurses, even for perhaps 10 million children on their homes. To ensure money to feed them through sickness and unemployment, they would in vain look for comfort from their working-class parents. Ninety-five children in every 100 were confined to state schools, often the nearest one round the corner. Many or most might be attended by local doctors employed by the state that replaced the Friendly Societies or other working-class insurance organisations. Perhaps a quarter of families lived in Council houses built by local governments which their parents could not improve.

Children saw these elements in private family lives as supplied by strangers over whose activities their parents had little or no influence.

Even worse: the poorer their parents, the weaker their cultural influence in pleading for better attention to the vulnerability of children with exceptional difficulties. And, worse than all the disabilities, the poorer children in the better state schools were displaced by children brought into the area by new higher-income residents who had moved to acquire the residential qualification required to use the local 'free' state schools and avoid paying fees for private schools. The parents, such as Mr and Mrs Blair, were doing their best for their children but at the expense of poorer children.

The strangers who replaced parents were often the members of the rent-seeking trade unions of teachers and professional associations of officials whose main purpose was to extract higher pay and better conditions from their local government employers rather than to satisfy parents that their children were educated to their satisfaction.

The usurpation of the authority of parents by 'public servants' weakened their family authority in other aspects of private and family lives. Not least was the observance of rules of personal conduct. The unwritten laws of the 'respectable working-classes' that I saw around me in the pre-war East End of London were being increasingly broken, often scorned, when post-war sociologists replaced parents as the teachers of civilised behaviour. The broken homes and personal unhappiness that followed the disparagement of marriage ignored the increasing evidence that children were happiest in households with two parents.

The dangers seem to have been seen by the new 1997 British Government: hence the emphasis of its March 1999 budget on easing the taxation of the conventional two-parent family. But there is a long way to go before the coherence of the family is restored by a revolutionary restoration of children's confidence in the capacity of their parents to ensure their well-being in the fundamentals of private lives.

Displacing 'Public' Officials

The ultimate solution is nothing less than the displacement of 'public' officials, 'public servants' and 'public' employees by the revival of the authority of parents to reject inadequate schools, crowded medical centres, and captive housing, and by empowering them to pay fees, medical insurance and rents or other costs. This is what parents will show they prefer as their incomes rise. Since many own homes with rising values that could produce neglected funds, they need no longer leave their children in the 'free' but no longer acceptable state schools or allow their lower-income parents to wait months or more for 'free' hip replacement or cataract surgery. The advancing 'working classes' may find new ways to pool their resources to strengthen family lives in defiance of the state that weakened them over the decades.

Public choice analysis reveals that the real public has little real choice precisely in the most personal services created by its representatives in government. The acceptance by politicians that they cannot satisfy the diversified requirements of the people – above all in education, medical care and their own homes – is the indispensable condition for the rejuvenation of British family life.

5

VOTERS VERSUS CONSUMERS

THE ANALYSIS OF PUBLIC CHOICE REVEALS, much more than conventional political theory, that collective choice-making in government has made the fundamental error of putting the vaguely identified interests of the people as voters before their clearly perceived interests as consumers. This historic error results in providing them with standardised services, supposedly to suit hundreds or thousands, or hundreds of thousands, or millions, rather than individuals or families in different circumstances with diverse preferences.

One-Size-Fits-All Services
The difference is between a tailor who supplies 'off the peg' one size, or six or 20 sizes, for thousands or millions of people instead of 'bespoke' sizes for each individual or family. Even where individual differences are deeply personal, the political process herds people into a few large pens in which they are treated as more or less equal or identical.

The suppression by government of individual judgement of the risks in everyday living is perhaps the most insensitive invasion of deeply individual liberty, where politically standardised treatment can do most harm.

Exploiting the Fear of Risks
Governments in Britain (and other democracies in Europe and North America) have exploited the human fear of risks in many regular or occasional decisions and purchases in everyday life. So it has offered 'help' in many forms, from advice to prohibition, in anxieties about loss of income in sickness, unemployment, old age and others. The new British Government is now going further, in paternalist or medieval-mercantilist manner, by arranging standards of quality or

precautions against uncertainty in a lengthening list of goods and services – food, clothing, motor-cars, homes and many others.

Its effects have varied from helpful to harmful. But its purpose has varied from winning popularity at elections to raising revenue in taxes to pay for services in which there is no public choice, and in principle no rejection.

Its most recent purpose – to raise taxes – reveals its fundamental internal tensions. Lately in Britain, perhaps because the 1997 government has exhibited increasing anxiety to protect consumers from imperfect or dangerous goods and services, the populace seems to be losing its faith in official advice. There is a new conflict between official advice from 'public' authorities and 'public' confidence in services chosen – or rejected – by individuals. A reason may be the accusations of critics that the goods and services at risk are those produced less by public-spirited 'public servants' than by 'profit-seeking' commercial companies. This distinction is difficult to maintain since the bulk of public complaint is directed to state-produced goods and services – poor schooling, inadequate medical care, poor housing. At the time of writing the most urgent public anxieties are directed at suspected unsafe foods. Here the evidence of national sample polling, imperfect though it often is in discovering 'public' opinion, reveals unprecedented loss of confidence in political judgement.

The findings may reflect the experience of disease evidently transferred from animals to humans in the early 1990s, but lately of special interest since the relevant poll was commissioned by the new government-created Better Regulation Task Force, in the praiseworthy task of assisting Ministers in 'managing risk'.

The object – to judge where to allow individual choice of risk and where to empower government to ban risks for all – seems laudable. The findings, which may be premature, seem to be that the politicians were not trusted by the public in judging where individuals could be left to judge risks themselves. They revealed a wide gap between the risks in foods publicised – or exaggerated – by politicians and as judged by scientists and other 'specialists'. The percentages of members of the public who reported anxiety conflict widely with the evidence of the scientists:

Risk	Public Anxiety	Scientific Evidence
1. Pesticides	69% (women)	No hard evidence
2. Genetically treated foods	57%	GM foods probably safer than many conventional foods
3. B.S.E. in beef	54%	Beef probably safe – no effects for years or decades
4. E. Coli	94% aware of risk 25% sense risk	Affects one in 46,000 in England
5. Salmonella	99% know the risk 51% sense the risk	Infection uncommon, rarely life-threatening
6. Camplyobacter	13% know the risk	Illness rarely fatal

Source: Daily Telegraph, 8 February 1999.

Clearly, public choice analysis indicates that politicians will not act strictly on scientists' findings. They will play safe and avoid the risk of blame for public anxiety at all costs. They will exaggerate the risks and hope to maximise the political goodwill. This is cheap political prudence since they can conceal the costs (taxes) of widespread precautions in masking the risks by complete prohibition of production or sale of the suspected substances. Suppressing the costs of insuring against the risks by well-publicised outright prohibitions is clearly preferred by the politicians. They stand to gain public goodwill at little or no cost to themselves in running government.

Yet it may be that people will, in the end, win the test of influence with the politicians. Government values people as voters more than as consumers. And the polls indicate increasing sophistication by the people as consumers (and producers) above their former selves as voters (and tax-payers).

The essence of the finding is not that government servants could not judge the chemical or other suspect content of risks in food. More fundamentally, the political objection is that politicians were not elected to judge risks collectively for the people as a whole, rather

165

than allowing individual people and families to judge risks for themselves.

Restraining Political Paternalism

Slowly, very slowly, the public is summoning its courage to tell politicians to restrain their self-interested paternalism – and in these days of increasing numbers of women in politics and especially the 1997 Parliament, maternalism. For to politicise the precautions against possible risks in food, and much else, is to pay scant respect to the common sense of the public and its better ability to judge whether the risks apply to those who take care in their choice of suppliers.

The government supervision of quality – in almost medieval-mercantilist detail – is an unseen cost of public choice that inflates the powers of 'representative' democracy which does not represent the better individual judgements of the people.

6

THE POLITICAL FATE OF

ECONOMIC FEDERALISM

Decentralising Government: The Case in Principle

THE PURPOSE OF FEDERALISM, outlined by Professor Tullock in Part I (and in his book, *The New Federalist*[1]), is to decentralise government and its political power as far as feasible to the smallest possible political authority which would be best acquainted with local circumstances and requirements. The economic result would be to leave the maximum possible amount of local economic activity to agreement among local individual residents or groups, and the minimum possible to control by the politicians.

The ideal outcome would be that economic functions – the public goods proper that could not be supplied by agreement between private individuals or groups – were performed by the most appropriate size of political governments. The supreme public good of prevention of friction or war between countries would be delegated to a small joint federal office, leaving most other functions to constituent countries and their local authorities.

Centralisation in Practice

The reality has been very different – in some countries almost the opposite. In the USA, and to a lesser extent in the other federal unions, Canada, Germany, Australia, political power has become more centralised because political decisions have been yielded to the federal government.

---

[1] G. Tullock, *The New Federalist*, Vancouver, BC: The Fraser Institute, 1994.

Public choice analysis, the economics of politics, reveals the main reasons for this disappointing outcome. In the light of this experience there is understandable anxiety in Britain about future developments in relationships with the countries of mainland Europe. For the British people this would be an unprecedented reform with undemonstrable advantages and unassessable risks. The analysis of public choice suggests probable developments in political structures and economic results that affect opposing arguments.

For the student of the economics of public choice the essential interest lies in the extent to which government creates the optimum size of political authority – centralised or decentralised – for the optimum economic functions. Professor Tullock has illustrated the optimum centralisation and decentralisation in the government provision of public services. Federal government is best confined to the few functions – the 'public goods' – most efficiently supplied from the federal centre for the 'federal' country as a whole. The more varied functions are best supplied by local agencies of government at the periphery which can take into account divergences in economic conditions and human preferences.

The Real World of Federalism

This is the ideal world in which political institutions are more, or, ideally, precisely suited to the varying geographical extent and similarity of economic functions. Here as elsewhere the ideal world and the real world differ widely. The real political world of federal systems has produced functions more centralised and more extensive than they need be and than the peoples would prefer and could create in free markets.

For the USA Professor Tullock has illustrated the many services that are better because they are more localised than in Britain. At the other extreme the US Federal Government has, over the decades, taken into its centralised control services that were once better controlled by the individual States.

The dangers of over-centralisation were seen in the creation of the Interstate Commerce Commission with the function (among others) of outlawing barriers, requested by importuning rent seekers, and created by State governments to exclude 'imports' from other States.

This aspect of internal trade in the USA – its tendency to impose protection from other 'countries' – is analysed in principle by Dr Brady in his discussion of 'protection'.

The Protection of Industry

The protection of industries was a growing feature of trade between the nationals of Europe until the First World War. One of the few arguable but plausible excuses exploited by Hitler in the Second World War was his complaint that the 1932 Ottawa Agreement excluded Germany from markets in Africa. It was one of the glories of the liberal school of scholars at the London School of Economics in the 1930s, led by Robbins and Beveridge and including names that should be remembered by the British people – F.C. Benham, A.L. Bowley, T.E. Gregory, J.R. Hicks, W.T. Layton, Arnold Plant, G.L. Schwartz – that in their 1931 testament, *Tariffs, The Case Examined*,[2] they openly deplored the abandonment of free trade and the adoption of protection. They signed their manifesto of faith in free trade by a declaration that echoes the nuances of the English language:

'…we should all think it a disaster, if the policy of Free Trade which has served Britain so well materially, as through her it has served as an inspiration to all who in any land have worked for good understanding among nations, were today to be sacrificed to ignorance or panic or jealousy or specious calculation of a moment's gain.'

One more reason for the growth of barriers to trade between individuals, families, firms or other private buyers and sellers emerged after 1931. The introduction of protection taught rent seekers in Britain and elsewhere that they could generate wealth for themselves more easily by importuning government to impose protection – by tariffs, quotas, and other devices – than by producing goods and

---

[2] *Tariffs: The Case Examined*; the authors were chaired by Sir William Beveridge, then Director of the London School of Economics, Longman Green & Co., Second and Popular Editions, 1932.

services wanted in open competition by the general population of consumers. Thus came about the modern growth of the rent seekers, whose origins, effects and damage to living standards are analysed in Part I by Professor Tullock.

Why Centralisation?

The important question is why the units – states and others – comprising countries called federal unions have allowed political power to become more centralised in the federal government rather than remaining decentralised in the separate units. Professor Tullock has indicated the economic advantages of decentralisation. The task for the economist is to explain why the economic advantages of decentralisation have been sacrificed in politically-inspired federal centralisation.

Here the economics of public choice offers explanations far superior to the unconvincing reasoning of outdated political science. Public choice is in essence based on the science of economics in everyday life transactions between real individuals or groups of people. Political science is largely limited to the study of the artefact machinery created by their supposed representatives in government. Economics dissects the advantages to individuals and groups in co-operating by purchase and sale of each other's goods and services – or lately on a small (but increasing) scale by barter.[3] Political science is largely limited to the study of the machinery of political government control over what would otherwise be private lives.

The tendency to centralisation of political influence in the North American Federal authority in Washington is of interest to the peoples of Europe. In Britain the focus of concern is how far economic integration in Europe will be exploited by the familiar fatal propensity of politicians to inflate their powers by centralising economic functions in larger units of political government approaching federalism.

Differences Between the USA and Europe

A comparison and contrast between the economic tendencies in the USA and Europe indicates similarities and differences that may

---

[3] A. Seldon, *The Dilemma of Democracy, op. cit.*

explain, though not necessarily justify, the differences in economic development and structure.

The 'new Europe' in the USA was created largely by Europeans from 'old Europe', but their economic and political developments have differed widely. Average income in the USA is 2.25 times that in Europe largely because of the size and the variety of the area in which there is internal freedom to trade, and therefore much wider scope for the specialisation ('division of labour') that, Adam Smith taught in 1776, is the secret of the production of wealth. The instinctive sense of Americans in all States, from the architects of the Union in the 1780s to the present day, was that the freedom to trade with the peoples of all other states in the union was the secret of creating a federal power that could prevent the parochial-minded state politicians from impoverishing the States by preventing inter-State commerce.

The acceptance of the USA Federal Union was also easy for the immigrants from Europe who since the early 17th century came from different countries – Holland, England, Scotland, France, Germany, Italy, Russia, Poland – yet who could accept one another as culturally comparable minorities. They soon learned that the wisest course was to exploit the differences between their skills and exchange their resulting products.

Great Britain was also the product of different, although only four, peoples: originally the English (formerly mainly Saxons and Danes) and the Welsh, in 1707 the Scots, and in 1922 the Northern Irish. They are now, at the meeting of the 20th and 21st centuries, decentralising some economic powers, mainly to the Scottish and the Welsh, but remaining a British, economically 'federal', union for joint services: defence, law and order and, so far, the social services of the welfare state. The intention was that joint functions would remain in the 'federal' (not so described) government in London. But many determined Scots want more power, exceeding the limited power to tax they now have, to act as an independent state in Europe.

The uncertainties, and anxieties for many British citizens, are how far economic union in Europe to ensure its original purpose – free trade to raise living standards – will evolve into a politically Federal union in which economic power to create, control or regulate working lives in Britain and the other countries in mainland Europe will be exercised by a 'Federal' government in Belgium or Luxembourg, with main institutions such as banking in France or Germany. Public choice, the essentially economic analysis of politics, is therefore a better guide than political science in assessing the probabilities.

The prospect for higher living standards in Europe with free trade has for some time been creating and multiplying producer interests that will organise as rent seekers to lobby the Federal authorities in mainland Europe even more than they have the national governments of their separate countries, and perhaps even more persistently than their long-experienced opposite numbers in Washington.

The further unknown is how far the combined countries of Europe may be tempted to act as a larger economic entity in its 'protective' relationship with the politically separate countries in other continents. A discouraging precedent is the recent abandonment by the once protectionist USA of its newer free trade mission in the World Trade Organisation.

European Producers and Rent Seeking

In Europe organised producers – in both employers' associations and employees' trade unions – have been learning the arts of rent seeking. The European Members of Parliament will be learning the arts of logrolling. The Ministers in the proposed European Union have been weighing the advantages of acting as national patriots against those of 'inter-national' European statesmen. The Common Agricultural Policy (CAP) will have taught the lessons of rent-seeking tactics and strategy. And the ruling Commissioners of the newly United Europe have lately been accused of the personal abuses of power familiar in other federal unions.

All these short-run calculations will be at the long-term expense of the interests of all the people – often ironically the same people – as individual and family consumers. Europe may emerge on a larger scale with the over-government that treats people cynically more as voters to enlarge the powers of the political masters than as the loyal servants of sovereign consumers.

These powerful (because immediate) short-term political impulses will contend with underlying long-term economic liberalism. The peoples of America retain fading European cultural loyalties of one or two centuries. The still nationally separate peoples of Europe continue with the cultural differences between North and South, East and West, of a thousand years. The uncertainty is whether the culturally-conscious people of Europe will accept as much Federal authority from Brussels or other capitals of the European Union as did their families who emigrated to America and are now proud of their second, third or fourth generations ruled from Washington.

Attitudes to Paying Taxes

Acceptance or rejection of government is fundamentally seen in the attitudes to paying taxes as they exceed acceptable limits and invade personal ability to raise living standards by mutually beneficial trade. There is a wide and decisive difference between accepting taxes with resignation and rejecting them with defiance. Professor Tullock has adopted a new term, 'tax avoision', for the mixture of legal avoidance and illegal evasion that tends to merge in law or is difficult to distinguish in moral content because government may be more immoral than the people if it imposes taxes that do not reflect their willingness to pay.

The official statistics of the national governments in Europe cannot be accepted as accurate measures of public approval. The experience of most individual countries reveals that the official figures of incomes, saving, employment or unemployment are vulnerable as measures of public approval. The official OECD figure of 18 million unemployed is a caricature of the real number of Europeans who may be officially 'unemployed' but are busy earning sizeable sums in all kinds of 'unofficial' work to keep their families in acceptable comfort.

And the more Europe is 'federalised' the less loyalty can be expected in the payment of European taxes or observance of European laws, rules or regulations. If the Italians, the Swedes or the Scottish resist taxes imposed in Rome, Stockholm or Edinburgh, they are hardly likely to be more scrupulous in paying taxes imposed in Brussels or Luxembourg.

Supplementary budgets, from annual to quarterly, to raise the missing revenue will multiply. Declarations of national revenue and expenditure at meetings of the G7 and other assemblies will become even more fictional.

The Rejection of Democratic Government

Democratic government is being rejected by more conventional methods of exchanging goods and services: from minor local forms of barter to larger-scale exchange of surplus stocks between sizeable companies. Electronic money in international exchange is also easing informal deals between strangers never likely to meet. These and other new means of exchanging valuable information or advice – commercial, legal, political, technical, medical and more – enable more people to bypass the over-arching intrusions of growing federal government. The assumption that governments supply services that are necessarily desirable is being questioned the more extensively they invade personal and family lives and the further they are from day-to-day activities – from local, through regional, to country-wide and federal origins.

Two conclusions follow, both from public choice analysis. The better prospects for the people, in their fundamental capacity as controllers of the use to which their resources are put, lies in the combination of economic system and political structure that places their economic authority as consumers in open markets before that as producers in the political arena. That authority will require a constitution that empowers them as tax-payers to discipline politicians by denying their taxes more than as voters who can less effectively deny their votes.

Escaping to Open Markets

The decisive conclusion is that the power of politicians to frustrate the people is not measured by the weight of legislation but more by the ability of people to escape from it in open markets. And the escapes are more numerous in federal systems misused to impose centralisation than in decentralised country, regional, and local government. Escapes are more numerous still in open market daily exchange between individuals who know one another's wants better than do 'public' servants.

7

THE ESCAPES FROM OVER-GOVERNMENT:
Political Power Yields to Economic Law

BEFORE BUCHANAN AND TULLOCK, THE PIONEER ECONOMISTS who initiated the invasion of politics by economic principles and revealed its pretence of devising the most democratic (because most representative) form of government, there were students of politics who sensed its limitations and dangers. But they fell short of analysing its structural imperfection and excesses.

Some Forerunners of Public Choice

Pierre Joseph Proudhon, the mid-19th-century French philosopher, but a weak economist, went too far. 'To be governed', he warned in 1857, 'means that at every transaction one is registered, taxed, priced, licensed, authorised, reformed, exploited, monopolised, robbed: all in the name of public utility and the general good.'

'Public' utility is the misleading description used by the political process to disguise the economic source of its superfluous services. Proudhon failed to distinguish between the unavoidable and the unnecessarily collectivised 'public goods' analysed by Adam Smith. Proudhon revealed his weak economics by listing pricing as an excess of government. It is largely the failure of government to price its growing services other than public goods that has produced over-government.

John Stuart Mill, the mid-19th-century economist, anticipated the claim that government would or could breed necessarily selfless benevolent politicians. Four years after Proudhon, when the two political parties, later labelled Conservative and Liberal, were contemplating a widening franchise from which they would extract increasing political support, Mill sobered expectations. Although he sat in the House of Commons as a Liberal for a few years he counselled:

> '...the very principle of constitutional government requires it to be assumed that political power will be abused to promote the particular purpose of the holder ... because such is the natural tendency ... to guard against which is the special use of free institutions'.

But such 'guarding' has not proved adequate in the century and a half since Mill. Constitutional (that is, representative) government has not protected the people against over-government. The old fallacy that only government can provide 'public services' has unnecessarily prevailed for a century or more. It lingers ironically in the British Liberal Party which was supposed to have disciplined over-government in its heyday of power in the late 19th century. After the March 1999 budget its financial spokesman, sadly a Scot who has probably not heard of Adam Smith, lamented the failure of the government and the Conservative Opposition to raise taxes in order to expand 'essential public services'.

It was left to the early 20th-century Austrian economist (and Finance Minister), Eugen von Böhm-Bawerk, to foresee, in his long 1913 essay, *Macht oder Ökonomisches Gesetz* ('Political Power or Economic Law'[1]), that government could and would over-reach itself by supplying services – not least education and medicine – that the citizens with rising incomes in the late 20th century could and ultimately did reject and escape in growing numbers. That is now the new trend in the function and content of representative government.

The Problem of Over-Government

It is nearing 40 years since the joint Buchanan-Tullock economic analysis of public choice revealed the unavoidable flaws in the belief

---

[1] Eugen von Böhm-Bawerk, 'Macht oder Ökonomisches Gesetz', first published in *Zeitschrift für Volkswirtschaft, Sozial Politik und Verwaltung*, Vienna, 1914.

that government should supply services that the citizen could buy in the market. The implication of the economic analysis of government is vital for the future of democracy and the rule of law. By its congenital failure to avoid over-government, and by inflating its powers and laws beyond the irreducible and therefore acceptable powers of government, democracy has endangered the rule of acceptable law.

The analysis of public choice can best be seen as the conflict within human beings in their functions as voters and consumers. Individual men and women do not consume simply what other men and women have produced. They produce what other men and women want as consumers. The study of public choice has revealed the fatal flaw that the political process has tended to pursue its own interests in siding with the people as producers rather than consumers.

Yet, as incomes rise, the primary power of the people lies increasingly in their economic ability as consumers to subordinate themselves as producers. The sad evidence of history is that the over-government produced by representative democracy has for a century and a half in Britain subjected the primary economic interest of individual men and women as consumers to their secondary economic interest as producers.

The Weakening Grip of Government

This power of government, especially since the end of the 1939–45 World War, is being radically weakened and undermined by changes in both arms of economic life – supply and demand. All human life is subsumed under one or the other. Demand is being gradually but massively transformed by rising incomes, changing methods of trading and exchange from selling and buying to barter, and the increasing use of electronic money. Supply is being dramatically transformed by technological advance, the move from office or factory to home, and the world-wide web. Trade between buyers and sellers has long been conducted between strangers linked indirectly by intermediaries – shopkeepers, wholesalers, shippers and more. The Internet is linking strangers living thousands of miles apart yet who can see and talk to each other. The Industrial Revolution in the simple mechanics of the 18th century is being surpassed by the transformed supply and demand of the magnified Market Revolution that began in the late 20th century and will grow exponentially in the 21st.

Not least, the notions among scholars, from economists to scientists, on the power of ideas over human action will have to change. The brightest intelligences teach that intellectuals can initiate political change. Politicians will have to accept with humility that their years of dominating human life are passing.

Means of Escape

One of the most recent developments is the exertion of market forces in humble family life to avoid, by escaping from, the politically determined inadequate financing of state education. Parents of children at state schools, ambitious for their future in the age of the computer, are not content with accepting the inadequate financing and technical equipment of the state schools. They not only increasingly pay fees. They also, after school hours, pay private tutors to teach their children the use of personal computers to ensure they are not handicapped in their later higher education opportunities and employment prospects.

The new British Prime Minister was coached to anticipate the coming technological revolution and early spoke of the guiding principle of his government to be 'Education, Education, Education'. He announced his arrangement with a leading technological company to equip all 25,000 state schools with 'free' computers – that is, without direct charge to parents. He did not mention their indirect payments by taxes, or their opportunity costs, for example by a host of delayed road improvements. The government-private enterprise compact will not be able to keep pace with the rate of advance and sophisticated variety of the new flood of innovations that the market will produce in the 21st century.

The intention of parents to better the prospects of their children will accelerate the long lead of the private schools over the state schools in teaching and equipping pupils for lives of work and fulfilment.

The extreme political outcome may be the demand of the egalitarian conscience that such 'offensive inequalities' be suppressed by government prohibition and regulation. The political process will be urged on by the rent seeking outlined by Professor Tullock and illustrated by Dr Brady for North America. In Britain rent seeking has long been exerted by the teacher trade unions, made powerful because the state has largely confined schooling to the state schools. But it will now lag behind the growing determination of parents with rising incomes to better the opportunities of their children for their lifetimes by making the best of their qualities.

In the larger canvas of the welfare state, not only in education, and not only between individual or groups of Members of Parliament, the two main political parties have in recent decades rolled each other's logs. With varying reluctance, and opposition from groups with long-term strategic outlooks rather than short-term tactical aims, the two main political parties have continued each other's policies. They have both overlooked the new powers of the people to escape from policies outdated by economic advance.

Government or Anarchy: Posing a False Choice
For three centuries thinking on the optimum role for government has been dominated by the belief, or fear, sown by Thomas Hobbes – that the alternative was anarchic chaos. That was not the alternative or the choice. The alternatives were not government or no government but too little or too much government. And for a century economists have attempted to define the boundary of acceptable government – neither too little nor too much – by analysing the extent of 'public goods'. The error, restated by the new British Minister of Social Services, Alastair Darling, was to suppose that government would not only supply them efficiently but that it would also withdraw from them as soon as they could be supplied by a choice of suppliers catering for individuals or families or small private groups with varying tastes.

This is the apotheosis of permanent politicised state welfare. It was the development of public choice which revealed the defects of collective supply and demand by government – the political process in which choices were expressed by the people with few choices as voters every few years rather than as consumers with numerous choices every day.

Thomas Hobbes, the 17th-century philosopher, in his notorious book *Leviathan*[2] (1650), confused thought on the nature of government that could ensure liberty and at the same time gave a powerful weapon to the advocates of big government down the centuries. Without 'sovereignty', he said, by which he meant strong government by the state, there would be chaos and anarchy.

But that was over three centuries ago. In the 21st century, political power will have to be exercised with more reticence and more respect for the common people. It will have to be used in deference to the sentiments of the populace who will have new powers to challenge the state. If government, as it now does, uses its powers to enact laws, rules, regulations and other commands that flout the sentiments of the people it will find they can escape as they never could before.

The 300-year-old warning of Hobbes, in a very different world, does not validate the excesses of collective 'public choice' that offend the real personal 'choices' of the real sovereign public in the new world of the 21st century.

---

[2] Thomas Hobbes, *Leviathan* (1650), Everyman's Library, London: J. M. Dent & Sons, 1924.

REFERENCES

Alchian, A. A., and W. R. Allen, *University Economics: Elements of Inquiry*, Belmont, CA: Wadsworth Publishing, 3rd edn., 1972.

Arrow, K. J., *Social Choice and Individual Values*, New York: John Wiley and Sons, 1951, rev. edn., 1963.

Bator, F., 'The Anatomy of Market Failure', *Quarterly Journal of Economics*, Vol. 72, August 1958, pp. 351–79.

Becker, G. S., 'A Theory of Social Interactions', *Journal of Political Economy*, Vol. 82, Nov./Dec. 1974.

Black, D., *The Theory of Committees and Elections*, Cambridge: Cambridge University Press, 1958.

Blundell, J., and C. Robinson, *Regulation Without the State*, Occasional Paper No. 109, London: Institute of Economic Affairs, 1999.

Buchanan, J. M., and G. Tullock, *The Calculus of Consent: Logical Foundations of a Constitutional Democracy*, Ann Arbor: University of Michigan Press, 1962.

Dahl, R. A., *A Preface to Democratic Theory*, Chicago: University of Chicago Press, 1956.

Downs, A., *An Economic Theory of Democracy*, New York: Harper and Brothers, 1957.

Friedman, M., *Capitalism and Freedom*, Chicago: University of Chicago Press, 1962.

Friedman, M., and R. Friedman, *Free to Choose*, New York: Harcourt Brace Jovanovich, 1979.

Harberger, A. C., 'Monopoly and Resource Allocation', *American Economic Review*, Vol. 44, May 1954, pp. 77–87.

Hayek, F. A., 'The Uses of Knowledge in Society', *American Economic Review*, Vol. 35, September 1945, pp. 519–30.

Hayek, F. A., *The Constitution of Liberty*, London: Routledge & Kegan Paul, 1960.

Hobbes, Thomas, *Leviathan, or the Matter, Forme, and Power of a Commonwealth Ecclesiastical and Civil*, New York: Macmillan Publishing Co., 1977; originally published in 1650.

Krueger, A. O., 'The Political Economy of Rent-Seeking Society', *American Economic Review*, Vol. 64, June 1974.

McKenzie, R. B., and G. Tullock, *The New World of Economics: Explorations into the Human Experience*, Homewood, IL: Richard D. Irwin, Inc., 1975, 2nd Edition, 1978, 3rd Edition, 1980, 4th Edition, 1984, 5th Edition 1988, 6th Edition, Retitled: *The Best of the New World of Economics...and Then Some*, 1988.

McKenzie, R., and G. Tullock, *Modern Political Economy: An Introduction to Economics*, New York: McGraw-Hill, 1978.

Mitchell, W. C., and R. T. Simmons, *Beyond Politics*, California: The Independent Institute, 1994.

Niskanen, W. A., Jr., *Bureaucracy and Representative Government*, Chicago: Aldine-Atherton, 1971.

Olson, M., *The Rise and Decline of Nations*, New Haven, CT: Yale University Press, 1982.

Olson, M., *The Logic of Collective Action*, Cambridge, MA: Harvard University Press, 1965.

Posner, R. A., 'The Social Costs of Monopoly and Regulation', *Journal of Political Economy*, Vol. 83 (4), August 1975, pp. 807–27.

Rowley, C. K., R. D. Tollison and G. Tullock (eds.), *The Political Economy of Rent Seeking*, Amsterdam: Kluwer Academic Publishers, 1989.

Rowley, C. K., W. Thorbecke and R. E. Wagner, *Trade Protection in the United States*, The Locke Institute, Edward Elgar, 1995.

Schelling, T. C., *The Strategy of Conflict*, Cambridge, MA: Harvard University Press, 1960.

Schumpeter, J. A., *Capitalism, Socialism and Democracy*, New York: Harper and Brothers, 1942.

Seldon, A., *The Retreat of the State*, Norwich: The Canterbury Press, 1999.

Seldon, A., *The Dilemma of Democracy: The Political Economics of Over-Government*, Hobart Paper No. 136, London: Institute of Economic Affairs, 1998.

Seldon, A., *The State is Rolling Back: Essays in Persuasion*, Economic and Literary Books, in association with The Institute of Economic Affairs, 1994.

Seldon, A., *Capitalism*, Oxford: Blackwell, 1990.

Seldon, A., *Socialism Explained*, London: Sherwood Press, 1983.

Smith, A., *An Inquiry into the Nature and Causes of the Wealth of Nations*, ed. by Edwin Cannan, Chicago: University of Chicago Press, 1976.

Tullock, G., *The Politics of Bureaucracy*, Washington D.C.: Public Affairs Press, 1965; University Press of America, 1987.

Tullock, G., *Toward a Mathematics of Politics*, Ann Arbor: University of Michigan Press, 1967, Paperback, 1972.

Tullock, G., *Private Wants, Public Means: An Economic Analysis of the Desirable Scope of Government*, New York: Basic Books, Inc., 1970, University Press of America, 1988.

Tullock, G., *The New Federalist*, Vancouver, B. C.: The Fraser Institute, 1994.

Tullock, G., *The Economics of Special Privilege and Rent Seeking*, Boston & Dordrecht, Netherlands: Kluwer Academic Publishers, 1989.

Tullock, G., *The Vote Motive*, with a British commentary by Morris Perlman, London: Institute of Economic Affairs, Hobart Paperback No. 9, 1976. Spanish Translation, 1980, Madrid, Spain: Espasa Calpe, S. A.; Translated by Maria Jesus Blanco; French Translation, *Le Marche Politique*, 1978, Paris, France: Association Pour L'Economie Des Institutions; Swedish Translation, *Den Politiska Marknaden*, 1983, Avesta, Sweden: Translated by Eric Jannersten; Italian Translation, *Scelte Pubbliche*, 1984, Florence, Italy: Le Monnier.

Tullock, G., 'The Welfare Costs of Tariffs, Monopolies and Theft', *Western Economic Journal*, Vol. 5, June 1967, pp. 224–32. Reprinted in Donald S. Watson (ed.), *Price Theory in Action: A Book of Readings*, Boston: Houghton Mifflin, 1969, pp. 201–07. Translated 'Los Costes en Bienestar de los Aranceles, Los Monopolioa y el Robo', *ICE* (January 1980), pp. 89–94. Reprinted in James M. Buchanan, Robert D. Tollison and Gordon Tullock (eds.), *Toward a Theory of the Rent-Seeking Society*, Texas A & M University Press, 1980, pp. 39–50. 'Reply', *Western Economic Journal*, 1968.

Tullock, G., 'Social Cost and Government Action', *American Economic Review*, Vol. 59, May 1969, pp. 189–97.

Tullock, G., 'Efficient Rent Seeking', in James M. Buchanan, Robert D. Tollison, and Gordon Tullock (eds.), *Toward a Theory of the Rent-Seeking Society*, College Station: Texas A & M University Press, 1980, pp. 97–112.

Tullock, G., 'Rent Seeking as a Negative-Sum Game', in James M. Buchanan, Robert D. Tollison and Gordon Tullock (eds.), *Toward a Theory of the Rent-Seeking Society*, College Station: Texas A & M University Press, 1982, pp. 16–36. Italian translation, *Scelte Pubbliche*, Florence, Italy: Le Monnier, 1985, pp. 261–84.

Tullock, G., 'Rent Seeking', in John Eatwell, Murray Milgate and Peter Newman (eds.), *The New Palgrave: A Dictionary of Economics*, London, New York, Tokyo: Macmillan Press, 1987.